Saudi Arabia:
A Modern Reader

Edited by Winberg Chai, Ph.D., D.H.L., D.L.

With best Wishes
Winberg Chai
May, 2005

UNIVERSITY OF INDIANAPOLIS PRESS
2005

Planning: Phylis Lan Lin, Executive Director, University of Indianapolis Press

Cover design and layout: Jeannine Allen

University of Indianapolis Press Advisory Board (2003–2005):
Shirley Bigna, Gerburg Garmann, Phylis Lan Lin, David Noble, Peter Noot, Philip Young

Printed in the United States of America

10 09 08 07 06 05   10 9 8 7 6 5 4 3 2 1

ISBN: 0-880938-59-5

Published by
University of Indianapolis Press
University of Indianapolis
1400 East Hanna Avenue
Indianapolis, IN 46227-3697

Fax: (317) 788-3480
E-mail: lin@uindy.edu
http://www.uindy.edu/universitypress

CONTENTS

INTRODUCTION
Winberg Chai

In spite of the current widespread debates now in progress in the media and among policymakers about the future American role in the Middle East after the U.S.-led invasion of Iraq in 2003, the general American public's knowledge about the region in general, and about the Kingdom of Saudi Arabia specifically, has been meager.

Saudi Arabia occupies four-fifths of the Arabian Peninsula with 865,000 square miles in the Middle East. The population was estimated in 2003 as 24,293,884 people with an annual growth rate of 3.5 percent. It has 257,504 billion barrels of oil in reserve, which is about 25.4 percent of the world's known oil reserves (as compared to the U.S., which contains about 2.6 percent of the world's oil reserves). It also has 180,355 trillion cubic feet of natural gas—a substantial additional energy reserve. As a result, Saudi Arabia plays a most influential role in shaping the outcome of the global economy. It also occupies a significant geopolitical importance as Saudi Arabia dominates the land mass between Asia and Africa. Most of the oil fueling the industrial economies of Europe, Japan, and the U.S. is transported in waters surrounding this peninsula.

Geography
Geographically, Saudi Arabia is bounded to the west by the Red Sea; to the north by Jordan, Iraq, and Kuwait; to the east by the Arabian Gulf, the United Arab Emirates, Qatar, Bahrain, and Oman; and to the south by the Republic of Yemen. The Red Sea washes a narrow strip of lowland whose width varies from ten to forty miles. These western coastal plains (called *Tihamats*) are unique in that they contain extensive marshlands and lava fields. To the east of these plains runs a range of mountains, interrupted periodically by valleys, known as *wadis*. The most important wadis with oases are al-Himdh, Yanbu, Famtima, and Itwid and Bisha, in the Asir region in the southwest. The Asir region also has the highest mountain peaks in the kingdom, rising to more than 2,743 meters.

The country's mountain ranges decline to the west, which is dominated by coastal plains. Floodwaters are thus able to wash silt onto these plains, making this soil amongst the most fertile in the country. The Mecca region ranges from mountains about 2,438 meters above sea level to 1,219 meters in the western Mahd al-Dhahab area, northeast of Jiddah, and to 914 meters in the Medina region.

The mountain ranges also extend to the northern part of the kingdom. The Najd plateau lies directly to the east of the northern section of the mountain range known as the Jabal Shammar. The plateau continues southward to Wadi ad-Dawaser and runs parallel to the Rub Al-Khali, with an average elevation ranging from 1,219 meters to 1,829. The Najd plateau's northern plains extend about 1,448 kilometers beyond Hail, the Rashidi capital, all the way to the Iraqi and Jordanian borders.

Most of Saudi Arabia, however, is a continuous sand desert, called the Rub Al-Khali; and as a result, water is the most scarce resource for both production and consumption activities. In fact, Saudi Arabia has no overland free-flowing fresh water source except when rains sometime flood valley regions. To make use of this water, the kingdom has constructed dams for irrigation and other industrial uses.

The climate and soil in certain regions are conducive to agricultural activity. These areas include Al-Hasa, Al-Qatif, Al-Qasim, Al-Aflaj, Al-Kharji, Jiz-Ran, Tihamak, Wadi Fatima, al-Medina, Taif, Abha, and Hail.

Thus, although Saudi Arabia is blessed with many natural energy resources, it must also contend with its harsh desert climate and lack of water resources.

History

Saudi Arabia is the homeland of the Arab people, and the first Arabs originated in the Arabian Peninsula. It is also the homeland of Islam (a word that literally means "surrender to the will of God"). Two of Islam's holiest sites lie within the kingdom; that is, the city of Mecca—where the prophet Mohammed in the year A.D. 632 rededicated an ancient shrine to Allah (the Arabic word for God) and required faithful Muslims to make a pilgrimage there at least once in their lives—and Medina, where the prophet Mohammed was buried. Muslims are taught their faith by reading the Koran (Quran), a book containing a series of revelations from God to the Prophet Mohammed. To Muslims, these revelations are the direct, literal word of Allah. From the beginning of the faith, however, the message of Islam was that belief alone was not sufficient to gain entry into paradise—one's life required action, social reform, and confrontation with evil. Therefore, a guardian is needed in order to fulfill Allah's command and to ensure that Muslims behave justly and honestly in society. As a result, Saudi Arabia has emerged as the guardian of the Islamic conscience and often is seen as the arbiter of Muslim values. This role of guardian is also the result of the fusion of Wahhabism and the Royal House of Saud.

To make a simple analogy, Wahhabism is to Islam what Puritanism is to Christianity. The name comes from Muhammed ibn abd al-Wahhab, a legal scholar and Islamic jurist who was born in central Arabia in 1703. He became a major force in Muslim intellectual history when in 1745, abd al-Wahab formed an alliance with Muhammad ibn Saud, the chief in the Najd region, and began a major reform and purification of Islam. For example, the Wahhab form of Islam emphasizes the puritanical concept of Unitarianism; that is, the oneness of God *(al Dawah al Tauhid)*. He preached a return to the orthodox practices of Muhammad's day and particularly condemned any devotion that detracted from the oneness of God. His interpretation of Islam was primarily based upon the works of the strict Hanbali scholar Taki al Din Ahmed ibn Taimiya. Thus, the Wahhab movement swept across the Arabian Peninsula, which at that time was not united under one kingdom but was home to many tribes and factions, who often fought amongst themselves. It must be noted that the term *Wahhabism* is not used in Saudi Arabia. Outsiders called them *Wahhabis.* A Saudi might use the phrase *ual dawah ibn al tauhid,* meaning, "the call to the doctrine of the oneness of God," to describe his faith.

The followers of Wahhabism marched out of central Arabia into western Arabia and Iraq. They captured Mecca and Medina, forced the Ottoman governor of Baghdad to accept an armistice, and then invaded Syria.

Their victories forced the powerful Ottoman government to respond militarily. Together with Muhammed Ali of Egypt, a viceroy of the Ottoman government in Cairo, the Ottoman's forces undertook an expedition against the Wahhabis. They managed to occupy Mecca and Medina and executed Saudi leaders and confined Wahhabism to the small oasis towns of central Arabia. This situation continued into the nineteenth century.

Turki ibn Abdul Allah organized troops to oust the Egyptians who had occupied the Najd. Turki protected the integrity of Saudi-Wahhabi rule, and now Wahhabism had become a nationalistic movement. Internal dissension ravaged the movement, however, when Turki was assassinated in 1834 by a rival within the family. Turki's son, Faisal, quickly picked up the reins of government.

In two decades, the stability caused by the tribal cohesion Faisal had built up ended in a series of civil wars between Faisal's sons, Abdul Allah and Saud. As a result of the dissension among the Saud family members, the rulers in Qatar and Behrain launched their own attacks as did other tribal leaders. In 1834, Muhammed Ali of Cairo broke with the Ottomans and decided to bring Arabia into his own sphere of influence. Faisal was forced to side with Cairo after his cousin, Kalid ibn Saud, was taken prisoner.

After Muhammed Ali's death in 1844, Adbul Allah escaped from prison and gained power for a period of several months, during which time power returned to the Saud family. Between 1875 and 1889, power changed hands between several of the brothers. Because of internecine fighting among brothers and sons, the Saud family was unprepared for the rise of power by the Rashidis, who had been put in power by the Sauds in Hail to govern the northern province of Jabal Shammar. Faisal's youngest son, Abdul al-Rahman, was forced out of Riyadh and exiled to Kuwait, along with his youngest son, Abdul Aziz ibn Saud. It was this son who would become the founder of the modern state of Saudi Arabia.

Abdul Aziz ibn Saud returned from Kuwait in 1902 and recaptured Riyadh. From this base, the Wahhabis resumed their campaign to wrest control of the Arabian Peninsula. Alliances with the Ottomans and with the British during World War I finally created the conditions necessary for the full conquest of the Arabian Peninsula by the Sauds. The British supported Abdul Aziz and a series of negotiations led to the treaty of Jiddah in 1927, which recognized Abdul Aziz's authority from the Gulf to the Red Sea while at the same time setting limits on expansion of his kingdom. In the same year, Abdul Aziz ibn Saud was crowned king of the Hejaz and Najd and their dependencies. He immediately established a consultative council, Shura (see Chapter 28, "The System of Government").

Abdul Aziz then began a balancing act of sorts between the forces of modernization and religious conservatism. In 1929, he established the Committee for Encouragement of Virtue and Discouragement of Vice, based upon long-standing Wahhabi practice, banning the drinking of alcohol as well as smoking, among other sins. At the same time, he promulgated the Organic Instructions of Hejaz, which guaranteed existing modern governmental institutions. Thus the government had two important facets: the secular political power of the king and the religious authority of the religious scholars (known as *ulama*), the *mutawwium* (which literally means "volunteers" but came to refer to the religious police or missionaries of Islam who made sure Islamic law was obeyed) and the king.

Finally, by 1930, Abdul Aziz was able to unify the various tribes of the Arabian Peninsula into what is now the Kingdom of Saudi Arabia and imposed upon them the austere principles of Wahhabism, which is now the ideological and social foundation of the kingdom.

Saudi Arabia's contacts with the Western world began after World War I. The first Saudi oil concession was awarded to Major Frank Holms of New Zealand, but he later sold it to Standard Oil of California (SOCAL). In 1933 SOCAL, with the help of British explorer H. St. John B. Philby and American Karl Twitchell, obtained new oil rights. SOCAL's subsidiary, the California Arabian Standard Oil Company (CASOC) was then created to prospect for oil in Saudi Arabia. In 1935, Saudi oil was discovered.

A year later, SOCAL joined with Texaco and took charge of Saudi operations. On January 31, 1944, CASOC's name was changed to the Arabian American Oil Company (Aramco). Four years later, Jersey Standard (Exxon) and Standard of New York (Mobil) also bought into Aramco, thereby making it a wholly owned subsidiary of four major American oil companies. (See Chapter 4.)

Between 1970 and 1973, the oil-producing countries of the world gained control over pricing from the companies. In December 1972, an agreement for 23 percent "participation" or equity was reached in several Gulf countries, including Saudi Arabia, and in June 1974, Aramco agreed to 60 percent Saudi participation. In March 1976, the Saudis gained 100 percent control of Aramco's remaining equity.

The social impact of the oil wealth on the kingdom was explosive, immediate, and beyond anyone's calculations at the time. For the first time in history, Saudi society was inundated with Westerners and their competing Western customs and languages. Gradually, the Saudis came to be part of two cultures: Arab and Western. With the accumulation of more oil money, there were also rising expectations and demand for social changes. Part Two of this book specifically covers these issues.

King Saud was unable to cope with these changes and was deposed in 1964. He was succeeded by his oldest brother, Faisal, who reorganized and modernized the Saudi government. For example, he abolished the institution of slavery and began major reforms to promote education and social welfare benefits for all Saudi citizens. He also sent his family and younger princes to study abroad including in the United States.

Unfortunately, King Faisal was assassinated by a deranged kinsman in 1975, and his brother, Prince Khalid, succeeded him. King Khalid died of a heart attack in 1982 and was succeeded by his half-brother, Prince Fahd bin Abdulaziz, a pro-Western modernist. He chose his half-brother, Abdulah, as crown prince. The crown prince became *de facto* ruler of the kingdom in 1996 after King Fahd suffered a stroke and continues in this role to the present day.

Society

Saudi society cannot be easily stratified into traditional categories of social and economic groups because of the interconnected relationships between different classes, tribes, and the royal family.

As stated earlier, because of its historical legacy as the location of the two most holy pilgrimage sites of Islam—Mecca and Medina—Saudi Arabia considers itself the guardian of Islam and Islamic values throughout the world. Islam is more than a religion; it is a way of life in the kingdom. Throughout history, the religious establishment was a partner in the administrative management of the Saudi state. The Al-Shaikh family of Addel-Wahab enjoyed continuous prestige and intermarried with the royal Al-Saud family. Even prominent ulama scholars who were not members of the Al-Shaikh family held influence, and the ulama enjoyed regular weekly meetings with the king and had direct access to the Majlis, the council that directed the state's affairs. Through their regular Friday sermons, the ulama have a public forum to question or support not only religious issues but also political and economic practices as well as their impact upon social values. The most influential members of Saudi society remain top members of the royal family. They are now active participants in all areas of society: government, military affairs, business, and educational enterprises.

As Saudi Arabia became more modernized in recent decades, technocrats and businessmen arose, forming a new middle class. The influence of this class no longer depends upon family origin, tribal connections, religious support, or other traditional qualifications. Instead, individuals' upward mobility depends most of all on their educational background, training, expertise, skills, and talent. One of the most prominent examples was Ahmad Zaki Yamani, who for many years was Saudi Arabia's Minister of Petroleum and Mineral Resources and who directly shaped Saudi oil policy. These new technocrats often have received their training outside the kingdom, in secular, mainly Western universities. In fact, many current ministers and deputy ministers in the Saudi government were educated in the United States. Together they are now the backbone of the kingdom's latest modernization efforts and create a pro-Western attitude within Saudi society.

Problems did develop and continue to develop within Saudi society, especially with the rapid growth of a youthful population and modernization. The most acute problems include housing shortages, unemployment, inflation, and pressure on social infrastructure as well as inequality in many areas for women. The new diversification policy of the Royal government is attempting to address these issues, however, by providing for increased industrialization of the economy, a new shift of the labor force toward the manufacturing sector, and efforts to provide advanced technological education to its citizens, male and female alike. For example, the government is increasing non-oil activities in the kingdom, including (1) manufacturing other than petroleum refining; (2) electricity, gas, and water production; (3) construction; (4) commerce, restaurants, and hotels; (5) service sector jobs; and (6) exploration to exploit other minerals in the kingdom. At present, however, the dominant force in the Saudi economy remains the production of oil.

From the point of view of growth, the amount that the country devotes to capital formation is significant. The Royal government continues to play a major role in sharing the wealth of the country with Saudi citizens. For example, the government provides subsidies for education and free healthcare, even including expensive transplant and experimental surgeries. This means that private consumption alone is not a sufficient measure of the economic welfare of the population.

U.S.–Saudi Relations

Historically, the U.S. and Saudi Arabia have been consistently close allies and friends, dating back to the days of President Franklin D. Roosevelt. (See Part One of this book for a complete history of this relationship as written by a retired U.S. diplomat-scholar.) Yet the American media often portrays Saudi Arabia oversimplistically as the hotbed of terrorism in the Middle East, occasionally reporting as though the Saudi kingdom were a primitive tribal state similar to Afghanistan. Another confusing aspect for the American people is the portrayal of Al-Qaeda sympathizers working within the kingdom to overthrow the Royal government because of its close ties to America. Rather than understanding that these terrorists are trying to disrupt Saudi society and its ties to the U.S., American television viewers may get the impression that it is the Saudi government itself responsible for these Al-Qaeda attacks, when in fact Al-Qaeda is adamantly opposed to the Royal government and wishes to turn Saudi Arabia into an even more fundamentalist and repressive religious regime, turning back all the modernization efforts—including new rights for women—to pre-twentieth-century conditions. (See Part Three of the book for more information.)

It is significant that President George H. W. Bush, in fact, delivered an address to the world in defense of Saudi Arabia on August 8, 1990 (see Chapter 7, "The Defense of Saudi Arabia"), in which he stated, "The sovereign independence of Saudi Arabia is of vital interest to the U.S." During the past decades, for example, more than 700 American companies have been engaged in business in Saudi Arabia. The enterprises involved extended to forty-two states in the U.S. These businesses cover virtually the entire spectrum of U.S. commerce—from weather stations to supermarket chains, tire manufacturing plants, shipbuilders, hospitals, fast food chains (including McDonald's®), hospitals, computer companies, and of course oil companies. Taken as a whole, the U.S. business relationship with Saudi Arabia has resulted in jobs for hundreds of thousands of American men and women and has had a positive and stabilizing influence toward a favorable U.S. balance of payment, in that the U.S. sells more to Saudi Arabia than the Saudis export to the U.S. in oil and other goods. Saudi Arabia also has invested billions of dollars in U.S. treasury bonds to stabilize the dollar and the U.S. economy. It is exactly this relationship that Al-Qaeda wants to destroy.

Thus, Saudi Arabia has decided to play a critical role in the current U.S. "war on terrorism." For detailed examples of extensive war aid from the Saudis, see the article reported by the Associated Press on April 25, 2004, and reprinted here as Chapter 26, entitled "Saudis Gave U.S. Extensive War Aid." Furthermore, Saudi Arabia secretly helped the U.S. during the 2003 Iraq War far more than the George W. Bush administration admitted publicly, including tens of millions of dollars in discounted oil, gas, and fuel. The kingdom also allowed cruise missiles fired from U.S. navy ships to cross Saudi air space to target Iraq.

This book is an introductory reader on Saudi Arabia. It includes four parts. Part One explores U.S.-Saudi Relations; Part Two discusses Saudi Arabian modernization; Part Three follows the War on Terrorism; and Part Four relates Saudi government information, interpretations, and statistics. All materials in this volume are compiled with permission from scholars, journalists, political leaders, and official government sources.

The editor's criteria for selection have been relevance and readability. The editor has tried not to abridge selections in order to maintain the sense of the original works. It is the editor's hope that the book will offer the reader an illuminating look at the fascinating portrait of the powerful forces of continuity and change at work in this most important country and U.S. ally in the Middle East today.

As readers can see from Part Two of this book, it was all but impossible for Saudi specialists to imagine the changes the world and the Kingdom would undergo over the past twenty-odd years. These chapters are provided specifically to give the reader historic perspective on the changes the kingdom has undergone from 1975 to 2005 and for comparative purposes with the current statistics and data provided in Part Four. It is the editor's hope that readers will examine these articles with the following questions in mind: What possible changes will the kingdom undergo in the next twenty years? How reliable are current pundits' predictions? What forces are currently at play in the Middle East and in U.S.-Saudi relations that will affect the region and the United States' relationship with Saudi Arabia in the twenty-first century? Where should our priorities lie as nations concerned with peace and stability?

Grateful acknowledgments are made for permission to reprint the materials in this book. (See Acknowledgment at the end of this book.) My thanks also to the editorial staff of the University of Indianapolis Press: its indefatigable director, Dr. Phylis Lan Lin; final editor R. Peter Noot, and its most conscientious editor, Katherine Murray, who carefully went over the entire manuscript multiple times.

PART ONE
U.S.–SAUDI RELATIONS

CHAPTER 1
Introduction to U.S. and Saudi Relations

Benson Lee Grayson

Of all the nations of the world, none today is of greater importance to the United States than the remote desert kingdom of Saudi Arabia. Despite its sparse population, which only recently has begun to abandon its nomadic way of life, the vast petroleum reserves located in Saudi Arabia have made America more dependent upon continued Saudi independence and good will than ever before relative to any country in our history. This fact was reflected in the declaration by President Ronald Reagan on October 1, 1981, that the United States would not permit Saudi Arabia to fall into the hands of any group, foreign or domestic, that would cut off the flow of Saudi oil to the West. Reagan's pronouncement, though (unlike a treaty) it had not received endorsement by the Senate, reflected as far-reaching a commitment as any American president has ever given for the defense of another country. [Cf President Bush's declaration in Chapter 7.]

The rapid emergence in the 1970s of a heavy dependence on the maintenance of friendly ties with the Saudi government has been one of the most significant and unexpected developments in modern American foreign relations. For most of its history, the United States possessed a degree of self-sufficiency unequaled among the great powers. Moreover, since World War I Americans have prided themselves on being citizens of the most powerful and wealthiest nation in the world. The growing dependence of the United States upon oil imports subject to the control of foreign governments has caused a shock to America's confidence and self-esteem from which we have still not recovered.

Today, the kingdom has emerged as the most important foreign source of American petroleum. Although imports from that country still constitute only a small part of America's total energy needs, as the biggest oil producer, Saudi Arabia's capability to increase production sharply and to market oil at prices significantly lower than that demanded by other producers has been a significant factor in enforcing a relative stability upon the world oil market and in helping to avert, at least temporarily, a world economic crisis. The importance of this situation to America cannot be overstated. Should the supply of petroleum from Saudi Arabia be interrupted, this nation's closest allies in NATO (North Atlantic Treaty Organization) and Japan would suffer such acute economic and attendant political harm that their continued association with the United States in defense of our joint interests would be open to question.

Under these circumstances, it is vital that United States policy toward Saudi Arabia receive the attention it deserves in this country and that it be formulated with full knowledge of what has gone before. Unfortunately, for most of the period of bilateral relations, that nation was deemed of little importance to the United States. American policy toward Saudi Arabia, so far as it existed, was decided by only a few individuals, with the general public being little involved. Today, that subject is of such concern to this country that the history of United States relations with Saudi Arabia should be familiar to all Americans interested in foreign affairs. Moreover, the officials of the United States government responsible for framing policy toward Saudi Arabia must possess a detailed knowledge of past developments between the two countries. Not only is there a far greater appreciation for the history of bilateral relations by the Saudis charged with such matters than among their American counterparts, but unlike the United States tendency to concentrate upon the events of the minute, the Saudis are prone to viewing current developments as they relate to those of the past and to the long-term future. This book is dedicated to helping to redress the lack of knowledge in the United States of past relations with Saudi Arabia.

CHAPTER 2
Early Relations

Benson Lee Grayson

Given today's extensive network of relationships between the United States and Saudi Arabia, it is ironic to consider how humble their beginnings were. A relatively new nation itself, America was a century and a half old when the Saudi Arabian state was established. The founder of the new nation was Ibn Saud (Abdul-Aziz Ibn Abdur-Rahman al-Faisal Al Saud), whose father held leadership of the puritanical Wahhabis sect and who signaled the coming resurgence of the family by capturing the area around Riyadh (the Nejd) in 1901. Ibn Saud initially looked to Great Britain for external support and succeeded in obtaining a subsidy from the British during World War I aimed at ensuring his cooperation against the Turks. It was the United States, however, with whom he eventually established close relations. In turn, Washington built its Saudi Arabian policy on the relationship with Ibn Saud and his successors, a condition continuing to the present day.

British policy toward the area that today constitutes Saudi Arabia was very muddled during World War I. The British authorities in India backed Ibn Saud and provided him with financial support. Simultaneously, the Foreign Office in London supported his rival, King Hussein, the Sharif of Mecca, with a larger subsidy and with an adviser in the person of the legendary Lawrence of Arabia. To make matters even more complex, the British government was at the same time secretly engaged in negotiations with France to partition the Ottoman Empire, obtaining primacy in Iraq and in return agreeing to recognize French influence over Syria and Lebanon. At the same time, the British promised to help establish a Jewish homeland in Palestine.

During these intricate maneuvers, the United States remained largely on the sidelines, as indeed did King Ibn Saud. Although American missionary activity had taken place along the periphery of Arabia—in Kuwait, Bahrain, Iraq, and Muscat in Oman—the interior of the Arabian peninsula remained virtually untouched, and American interest in that area all but nonexistent. As the war went on, Britain gradually concentrated its support behind King Hussein, who proclaimed himself king of Hejaz. At the Versailles Peace Conference, President

Woodrow Wilson accepted the recommendation of Britain and France that the delegation representing Hejaz, led by Hussein's son Emir Feisal and including Colonel Lawrence as an advisor, be admitted to the sessions.[1]

In March 1924, Britain shortsightedly terminated its subsidy to Ibn Saud. No longer having a financial incentive to follow British advice to maintain the status quo in Arabia and recognizing that the Hashemite administration in Hejaz had little popular backing, Ibn Saud overthrew it, occupying the holy city of Mecca and uniting Hejaz with the Nejd. In 1926, he had himself proclaimed king of Hejaz and Nejd.

Having unified his country, Ibn Saud now sought international recognition. On September 28, 1928, the Foreign Ministry of the kingdom notified the State Department—directly and via the American Legation in Cairo—of its interest in obtaining diplomatic recognition from the United States. Secretary of State Frank Kellogg, speaking for the Coolidge administration, responded in friendly fashion but declared that the time was not right for giving an affirmative reply.[2] Although Great Britain had signed a treaty with Ibn Saud in 1927 recognizing Saudi independence, other diplomatic recognition was scant. Moreover, the borders of the nation were still in question, and the lack of American ties to the area made the United States loath to take what might have been a premature move in recognizing the regime.

By February 1931, however, the U.S. State Department considered that the time had come to establish relations with the king. In part this shift in attitude was prompted by the fact that Ibn Saud had obtained recognition from an increasing number of nations, including Germany, Persia (Iran), and Turkey. An additional factor was the recommendation by the American Legation in Cairo that this step be considered. The suggestion stemmed from conversations between the minister and Harry St. John Philby, a former British Foreign Office official who had established close personal ties with Ibn Saud and become a Moslem and a permanent resident of Jidda. After some delay occasioned by the belief that relations with the Kingdom of Hejaz and Nejd should be initiated at the same time as with Iraq and Yemen, Washington on February 10, 1931, instructed the American ambassador in London, Charles G. Dawes, to inform the Hejazi minister there that the United States was now willing to hold discussions in London concerning the establishment of relations.[3]

The locale chosen was as a result of the fact that the Hejazi minister had participated in earlier discussions of the matter with the American Legation in Cairo while serving in Egypt. Additionally, the Foreign Office at that time had far greater information on conditions in the Middle East than was available to the State Department. Dawes was asked to request the British government to furnish him with any confidential information they believed might affect an American decision concerning the question of recognizing Ibn Saud's government.

Negotiations in London did not take long. On May 1, 1931, the United States extended full diplomatic recognition to the government of the Hejaz and Nedj and asked the Hejazi minister in London to communicate that fact to his Foreign Office in Mecca. In accordance with its normal policy, the State Department concurrently sought to conclude a treaty of friendship, commerce, and navigation to accompany the establishment of relations, which was signed in London on November 7, 1933, and went into effect the same day. The agreement was unexceptional, giving both parties "most favored nation" status. Some delay was caused, however, by the Saudi government's refusal to include language that could be interpreted as giving non-Moslem American consular officials the right to visit Moslem holy places or the right to free slaves. (The Royal negotiator feared that American officials might claim this right under the "most favored nation" status by asserting that it was held by British consular officials in the country as a result of murky historical precedents.) In the interim between the accordance of recognition and the signing of the friendship treaty, the name of the Kingdom of the Hejaz and Nedj was formally changed in September 1932 to the Kingdom of Saudi Arabia, and it was under this designation that the Saudis signed the 1933 agreement.[4]

Despite the conclusion of the treaty and the formal recognition of Saudi Arabia, the United States did not immediately establish a permanent diplomatic presence in that country. Commercial relations between the two nations were still minimal.

The world economic depression made the administration of President Franklin Roosevelt, which took office in March 1933, reluctant to bear the cost of opening a legation in Jidda, the diplomatic capital. Finally, the State Department feared that the king's suspicions of normal diplomatic procedures would prevent a resident legation from accomplishing anything significant. In the absence of a permanent mission, the limited American interests in Saudi Arabia that existed were handled by the United States Legation in Cairo. In 1936, Leland Morris, the American Consul General in Alexandria, Egypt, visited Jidda to investigate conditions and to furnish recommendations to the State Department as to whether it would be desirable to establish an official American representation in Saudi Arabia. His report, submitted in March 1937, concluded that the level of American interests did not warrant the establishment of any sort of mission in Jidda at that time.[5]

If the level of American-Saudi Arabian relations in 1936 gave scant indication of the close ties that would later develop, the first clouds of a storm that would one day seriously strain bilateral ties between the two nations were already appearing on the horizon. In April 1936 disorder broke out between Jews and Arabs in the British-administered Palestine Mandate. London, shocked by the loss of life and obliged to rush additional troops to Palestine to restore order, appointed a Royal Commission to determine the causes of the violence and to ascertain whether the Jews or Arabs had a legitimate reason for questioning the manner in which the Mandate was being implemented.

The Roosevelt administration was under strong pressure from pro-Zionist groups in the United States favoring creation of a Jewish homeland in Palestine to intervene in the situation and particularly to use its influence to ensure that the flow of Jewish immigrants to Palestine from Europe was not impeded. Responding to this pressure, on July 7, 1937, Secretary of State Cordell Hull telegraphed the American ambassador in London to advise him of the American government's interest in the problem and to remind him that every United States president beginning with Woodrow Wilson had expressed his support for the creation of a Jewish homeland in Palestine.[6]

It would have been hard to find a subject more likely to incur Saudi enmity toward the United States than the position taken by Washington on the Palestine issue. Not only was Ibn Saud involved with Iraq and other Moslem nations to support the Arab position in Palestine but, then as now, the Saudi government looked upon its administration of the Moslem holy cities as giving it a leading role in championing the cause of Arab nationalism and independence. Again, then as now, American oil interests in Saudi Arabia could be held hostage to pressure Washington on this matter.

On July 12, 1937, James A. Moffett, the chairman of the Bahrein Petroleum Company, Ltd., a subsidiary of the Standard Oil Company of California having a concession in Saudi Arabia, called at the State Department to make known his concerns. Recalling that King Ibn Saud had heretofore been friendly to American interests, the chairman noted that the company's representatives suspected the king was exhibiting a less cooperative attitude toward the Americans coupled with a growing tendency to work with the British. Moffett warned that any disposition by Washington to support Jewish claims in Palestine could have serious repercussions on American oil interests in Saudi Arabia and might even result in their expulsion.[7] The United States was then not dependent upon imported oil. The State Department's response to this approach was confined to an expression of thanks at being kept informed of the situation in the kingdom and assurances that the United States government was not officially involved in the Palestine dispute and had not taken any official position on the issue. Nonetheless, the linkage of Saudi oil to a favorable American attitude with regard to Saudi foreign policy objectives was a signal of things to come.

The importance Saudi Arabia attached to the Arab cause in Palestine was conveyed directly to the United States in December 1938 by means of a letter from King Ibn Saud to President Roosevelt. Transmitted via the American Legation in Cairo, the letter stated that the American people had been grossly misled concerning the Palestine situation because of widespread Jewish propaganda. The letter added that the Arabs had a greater historical claim to Palestine than had the Jews and that the stream of Jewish immigration into that region was threatening the rights and property of the Arab inhabitants.[8]

The king's letter caused a major review of American policy toward Saudi Arabia. Commenting to President Roosevelt in a memorandum dated January 9, 1939, Undersecretary of State Sumner Welles noted that it was the first complaint by an Arab chief of state to Washington that the United States had taken a position favoring the Zionist cause. The undersecretary stressed the importance of the king, describing him as the outstanding Arab ruler and as the person most qualified to speak on behalf of the Arab people. For these reasons, Welles recommended that more than a perfunctory reply be made to Ibn Saud. President Roosevelt concurred and the formal American response, presented to the Saudi charge in Cairo on February 15, 1939, was warmly worded.[9] In an effort to reassure the monarch that the United States was not intervening to support creation of a Jewish homeland, the reply indicated that although the United States in principle favored a Jewish homeland, only Great Britain had the responsibility for determining the procedures under which it administered the Mandate.

Although the United States did not significantly alter its position on Palestine because of the Saudi pressure or because of the American oil concessions in Saudi Arabia, the latter led to the American decision to establish a diplomatic representation in that country. In May 1939 the State Department notified Bert Fish, the American minister in Cairo, that it was considering the question. Washington's interest in establishing a diplomatic presence was as a result of the fact that the number of American citizens residing in Saudi Arabia had risen to 273, of whom 263 were employees of the Standard Oil Company of California subsidiary. Additionally, the Japanese government appeared likely to accredit its minister in Cairo to Saudi Arabia as well, and the State Department believed that it might concurrently accredit Fish as minister to Saudi Arabia while he continued to reside in the Egyptian capital.[10]

Fish agreed with the proposal, notifying the State Department that the number of Americans in Saudi Arabia had risen still further to more than 325, and that American and other foreign investment in the country had materially increased. Fish added, however, that the primary factor in his decision was the oil one, as California Standard Oil Company had recently obtained an exclusive concession covering almost all of Saudi Arabia for a period of sixty years. During the process of negotiating the concession with the oil company, the monarch told a company official that he had chosen the U.S. over the competing Japanese and British firms, even though the latter had offered greater sums for smaller concessions, to strengthen the American presence in his country. Fish informed the State Department that he agreed with the California Standard Oil Company's request that a legation be established in Saudi Arabia so that the interests of the firm could be safeguarded.[11]

Fish was a political appointee rather than a career diplomat (he had been serving as a judge in Florida when named to be minister in Cairo by the incoming Roosevelt administration), but his views were nonetheless valued within the State Department. Additionally, his recommendation was backed by the American minister in Iraq, who advised Washington that the proven importance of American oil interests in Saudi Arabia and the generally improved economic conditions that would result from this made it desirable that the United States establish a diplomatic presence. In July 1939 Secretary of State Hull obtained President Roosevelt's agreement to accrediti Fish to the Saudi government, citing the recommendations from the ministers in Cairo and Baghdad and pointing out that it would cost no additional expense beyond the nominal sum involved in Fish's travel between Cairo and Jidda. On August 3, 1939, the Senate confirmed Fish's nomination as minister to Saudi Arabia, and he traveled to Jidda and presented his credentials to King Ibn Saud on February 4, 1940.

The arrival of the first American minister to Saudi Arabia thus lagged behind the start of American commercial ties with that country by almost ten years. The lead in interesting United States firms in dealings with Saudi Arabia had been taken [by Saudi Arabia] in part because of the great world depression, which caused a drying up of the flow of religious Moslems making the pilgrimage to Mecca and Medina and forced Ibn Saud to search for other sources of revenue. The king hoped that valuable mineral deposits might be found in Saudi Arabia, but in 1928 a British firm that had obtained a concession to explore for oil allowed it to lapse in the belief that no commercially exploitable deposits existed there.

At this juncture Harry St. John Philby, who had earlier helped to broker the American recognition of the Saudi government, volunteered to help attract American commercial interest in Saudi Arabia.[12] Fortunately for the Saudis, opportunity knocked at the door in the person of Charles R. Crane, a wealthy industrialist and diplomat, whose father had founded the Crane plumbing supply company of Chicago. After serving as minister to China under President William Howard Taft and as a member of the American delegation to the Versailles Conference, he was again named minister to China by President Woodrow Wilson in 1920. During the Versailles discussions, Crane had helped draft a report on the former Turkish territories in the Middle East and, becoming interested in the area, he unsuccessfully attempted to meet King Ibn Saud in a visit to Jidda in 1926. Several years later, while traveling by from Basra to Kuwait, Crane narrowly escaped death at the hands of an irregular [unofficial] Saudi raiding force crossing the Iraqi border to loot.

In 1930 Crane visited Yemen to explore commercial possibilities there and accepted an invitation to visit Jidda to meet with the king. His discussions with Ibn Saud and Philby in May 1931 went well, and Crane expressed interest in further exploration work in Saudi Arabia to look for oil and in examining the possibility of resuming operations in an abandoned gold mine at Mahd al Dhahab, approximately eighty miles southeast of Medina. According to legend, the mine had been operated by King Solomon. Crane agreed to finance survey work for six months by Karl S. Twitchell, a mining engineer who had been associated with Crane in Yemen.[13]

For Twitchell, a native of Vermont who had helped to operate the British copper mines in Cyprus during World War I, it was the start of a long association with Saudi Arabia as an engineer, consultant, and author. After several months of fieldwork, Twitchell informed the Saudi government that although the limited underground water supplies in the Hejaz gave scant promise of being able to support expanded agriculture desired by the king, the gold mine at Mahd al Dhahab appeared to be commercially exploitable. Even more important for Saudi Arabia's future, Twitchell found what he believed to be a promising area for oil exploration at Dhahran, on the Persian Gulf.

Returning to the United States to persuade American firms to invest in Saudi Arabia, Twitchell met with officials of the Standard Oil Company of California. Despite the world depression, the company was seeking to expand its overseas oil reserves and had already located oil in its concession at Bahrain. The company hired Twitchell to act as one of its representatives in dealing with the Saudis. Together with Lloyd Hamilton, another company official, he worked out an agreement for the American firm to be given an oil concession in Saudi Arabia, which was signed by the Saudi Minister of Finance in May 1933.

The concession, some 360,000 square miles, was one of the largest in the world. Standard Oil of California was aided in its negotiations by the fact that it was employing Twitchell, who was highly regarded by Ibn Saud, and was supported by the good offices of Philby, who was even more favored by the king. Again, the company moved adroitly to provide Ibn Saud with a down payment of gold specified in the agreement. Although the Roosevelt administration had taken the United States off the gold standard in 1933 and American firms were legally banned from dealing in it, the company acquired the required gold to meet the Saudi payment from abroad when it was unable to do so in the United States.

The Arabian oil concession was assigned by Standard Oil Company of California to a subsidiary, the California Arabian Standard Oil Company (Casco). In 1936 another American firm, the Texas Company, purchased a half-interest in Casco. After initial failures, Casco made a major oil discovery in March 1938. As noted previously, the expansion of American official interest in Saudi Arabia generally paralleled the growth of the oil industry there. Both were to become increasingly important as World War II approached.

ENDNOTES

1. United States Department of State, *Foreign Relations of the United States* (hereafter *Foreign Relations*), *The Paris Peace Conference, 1919,* Washington, D.C., 1943, Vol. III, p. 599.

2. *Foreign Relations, 1930,* Washington, D.C., 1945, Vol. III, p. 282.

3. *Foreign Relations, 1931,* Washington, D.C., 1946, Vol. II, pp. 547-550.

4. *Foreign Relations, 1933,* Washington, D.C., 1949, Vol. II, pp. 989-991.

5. *Foreign Relations, 1939,* Washington, D.C., 1955, Vol. IV, p. 824.

6. *Foreign Relations, 1937,* Washington, D.C., 1954, Vol. II, p. 890.

7. *Ibid.,* p. 893.

8. *Foreign Relations, 1938,* Washington, D.C., 1955, Vol. II, pp. 994-998.

9. *Foreign Relations, 1939,* Washington, D.C., 1955, Vol. IV, pp. 694-696.

10. *Ibid.,* pp. 824-825.

11. *Ibid.,* pp. 826-827.

12. See Philby, Harry St. John, *Saudi Arabia,* NY and London: Benn, 1955.

13. See Twitchell, Karl S. *Saudi Arabia,* Princeton, NJ: Princeton University Press, 1958.

CHAPTER 3
World War II

Benson Lee Grayson

World War II, which caused so many changes in the world, had a pronounced effect upon American-Saudi Arabian relations. Its initial impact was to cause economic hardship for Ibn Saud's government, because the conflict greatly curtailed the flow of pilgrims to Mecca and Medina, upon which much of the Saudi economy was based. At the same time, exports of Saudi petroleum were reduced by the efforts of both the Allies and the Axis powers to cut off supplies to the other. Moreover, as the war continued, the American and European experts who had previously provided technical advice and assistance to Saudi Arabia in a wide range of areas became increasingly unavailable.

To satisfy his financial needs, the king turned to Britain and the United States. Saudi Arabia had early declared its neutrality in the war, but many of the Arab nationals favored an Axis victory as more likely to result in the independence of the Arab-occupied regions under British and French administration. Great Britain therefore provided limited financial assistance to Ibn Saud to maintain his friendship and to ensure that he continued his pro-Allied stance. At the same time, Britain's financial resources were limited compared to the massive wartime requirements that existed, and its need for oil was satisfactorily met from Iran to Iraq, without recourse of Saudi supplies. Accordingly, Great Britain informed the king that it could not meet all his requirements, prompting him to turn to the California Arabian Standard Oil Company for help.

On April 9, 1941, James A. Moffett, representing the California Arabian Standard Oil Company, met with President Roosevelt to advise him that the Saudis had asked his company to provide financial assistance. In a follow-up memorandum, Moffett stressed to the president that Ibn Saud was in a difficult financial position because of the war, that he had indicated his sympathy for the Allies, and that he needed $10 million a year for the duration of the war-induced crisis. To meet the king's demand that the Casco Company furnish him with $6 million in 1941, Moffett proposed that the United States assist the firm by purchasing from $6 million in petroleum products from the Saudi government, thus relieving Casco of the need to directly provide the sum. Moffett felt that this request was justified by the fact that Casco had already invested approximately $27.5 million in developing the oil concession in addition to another $6.8 million advanced the king against future oil royalties, that it had discovered an estimated 750 million barrels of oil, and that the two American companies jointly owning Casco had approximately 160,000 American stockholders.[1]

The Roosevelt administration carefully investigated the plan proposed by Moffett, ignoring political or strategic consideration, and ultimately rejected it for technical reasons. Secretary of the Navy Frank Knox informed President Roosevelt on May 20, 1941, that he had looked into the quality of Saudi oil and had found that it was not suitable for Navy use. Jesse Jones, the Federal Loan Administrator, was next asked to find some means of furnishing financial assistance to the monarchy. He, too, was unable to comply. He advised the secretary of state on August 6, 1941, that he had studied the matter but had been unable to find any authority for the Reconstruction Finance Corporation that he headed to give money to Saudi Arabia or to purchase oil in the ground in that country.

Although these technical difficulties were important factors in the ultimate American decision to turn down the Calso proposals, the most important criteria was probably the administration's view that Saudi Arabia was more an area of British concern than American. In May 1941, Secretary Hull transmitted to Viscount Halifax, the British ambassador in Washington, the information on Saudi Arabia's financial difficulties obtained from Moffett, with the implication that London might wish to alleviate them. Subsequently, London increased its grant to the king by some $800,000, to a total of $4 million, and asked the State Department if it could also contribute funds for this purpose.

The United States, however, did not want to become directly involved in providing the aid to Saudi Arabia. Rather, President Roosevelt suggested to Jones, who in turn passed the information on to the British Treasury representative in America, that Great Britain might want to meet Ibn Saud's request for funds out of the $425-million loan that the administration had just granted Britain. The American reaction to the Saudi request for direct aid was transmitted on August 22, 1941, to the United States minister in Cairo, for delivery to the Saudi minister there. The American note expressed the highest appreciation for the achievements of King Ibn Saud and stressed that the continued independence and well-being of Saudi Arabia were of great importance to the United States. However, the American government believed it had to devote its main efforts to assisting those countries that were actively resisting aggression, or which for geographical reasons were important to defense. Moreover, this country was furnishing considerable assistance to Britain, with whom the United States was sharing the effort of aiding nations resisting the Axis, and Britain had already given financial assistance to Saudi Arabia.

Saudi Arabia, indeed, was neutral in the war, although Italian aircraft had dropped some bombs on the Casco oil installations at Dhahran in a raid in October 1940, causing many of the Americans to return to the United States and contributing to a decline in oil production. The Roosevelt administration thus had a pretext for providing aid to Saudi Arabia if it had wanted to do so. In retrospect it seems strange that rather than seeking the goodwill it would have obtained in the kingdom by proffering the relatively modest funds requested, the United States preferred to have Britain gain the appreciation of the Saudis in making available to them what was in essence American money.

The brush-off being given the Saudi request was protested by Alexander C. Kirk, a career diplomat who had succeeded Bert Fish as American minister to Egypt and to Saudi Arabia in February 1941. Kirk urged on August 30, 1941, that the proposed American reply be revised. He warned that the language in the proposed response concerning a division of effort between the British and American governments would lead the Saudis to believe that Washington had resigned to the British all initiative in the Near East generally and in Saudi Arabia in particular. Further, the inference that the Saudis were inactive in the war would be regarded by Ibn Saud as gratuitously offensive because Saudi Arabia had used its moral influence with the other Arab nations to help keep them from falling under Axis influence.

Kirk's arguments were overruled by the secretary of state, who informed him on September 10, 1941, that the decision not to grant credits to Saudi Arabia had been made on the actual merits of the case and had been taken despite the British recommendation that American financial assistance be provided. And, as the crusher, Kirk was informed that it was the considered view of President Roosevelt that financial aid to Saudi Arabia would take the United States too far afield and that Great Britain had more reason than this country to look after Saudi financial needs.[2]

Fortunately, there existed an opportunity for the United States to show its goodwill toward Saudi Arabia at no great cost. In November 1940, Karl Twitchell, acting as informal representative for King Ibn Saud, transmitted to the State Department a request from the king that it make available the services of competent American road engineers, later broadened to include agricultural advisers. Twitchell also called upon the British embassy in Washington, which lent its support in urging the State Department to accede to the request, additionally proposing that Twitchell himself head the American mission.

The State Department agreed with the idea. In a message to Kirk on June 20, 1941, asking for his recommendations, the State Department pointed out that placing a small group of American agricultural and engineering experts at Ibn Saud's disposal for as long as might be necessary to complete their survey and prepare a report would be a gesture America could easily make. Moreover, this would not require the establishment of a permanent office in Jidda, which political considerations might make it difficult to withdraw if it were no longer needed.

Kirk agreed that some gesture of goodwill toward Saudi Arabia was desirable. Before the Saudi request could be granted, however, the country withdrew its request for the experts, probably because it was unwilling to pay the dollar costs involved while its financial difficulties continued. The United States nonetheless continued to review the plan, regarding it as a convenient method of cushioning the effect of its rejection of the Saudi request for financial aid. On September 26, 1941, the State Department cabled Kirk in Cairo that it desired to do anything that could be done to lessen King Ibn Saud's inevitable disappointment over the American decision not to extend assistance. Accordingly, Kirk was instructed to notify the king informally during a forthcoming visit to Jidda that the United States would be pleased to send a group of engineering and agricultural experts if requested. The State Department message added that the British minister in Jidda strongly supported the proposal and that the cost of the mission could be met by President Roosevelt's emergency funds for handling matters affecting American national security.[3]

The direct United States involvement in World War II greatly reduced Washington's reluctance to seek closer ties with Saudi Arabia. On February 10, 1942, President Roosevelt told Undersecretary of State Summer Welles of his desire to establish a permanent legation there, with Kirk remaining as minister accredited to both Egypt and Saudi Arabia but with a charge and a small staff residing permanently in Jidda. Saudi approval was quickly obtained, and on April 22, 1942, James S. Moose, a career Foreign Service officer, arrived in Jidda to open the legation. The State Department also moved rapidly to dispatch the proposed engineering and agricultural experts to Saudi Arabia, Twitchell being named to head the mission.

A major reason for the new American concern with Saudi sensitivities was Washington's consideration of a plan to construct one or more American Army airfields in Saudi Arabia. Secretary of State Hull informed Kirk on February 6, 1942, that President Roosevelt would send an appropriate letter to King Ibn Saud, using as the occasion the Twitchell mission. Six days later, Undersecretary Welles gave the president a note for him to send to the king. Welles advised Roosevelt that the message and mission would have a thoroughly favorable effect upon Ibn Saud, whom he described as the most influential figure in the Arab and Moslem world generally. The undersecretary also pointed out the potential importance to America of air bases in Saudi Arabia, commenting that the United States might need to acquire extensive facilities in that country to prosecute the war.

Accepting Welles' recommendation, President Roosevelt on February 13, 1942, signed the warmly worded letter to the king. It stated that the United States recognized that the war had upset the normal economy of Saudi Arabia and would pay the salaries and expenses of the Twitchell mission. To prepare the way for a possible later request for the airfields, the president's message also referred to the need to destroy the "evil forces" of Germany, Italy, and Japan, and expressed confidence that the king would assist in an appropriate manner.[4]

Kirk traveled to Saudi Arabia in mid-May 1942 to present his credentials formally to the king, at the same time delivering the president's letter and introducing the members of Twitchell's mission. All of these approaches were warmly welcomed by the Saudis. The king went out of his way to demonstrate high regard for the United States and for the American minister. In a note to President Roosevelt dated May 13, 1942, Ibn Saud expressed his pleasure at the president's letter and at the arrival of the Twitchell mission. He further implied his willingness to give more concrete help to the United States war effort, stating that he hoped that permanent peace might result from the conflict then in process, and that every responsible person had the duty to contribute toward this end.

The War Department had assigned an Army officer to accompany Kirk's party with the mission of investigating the practicality of establishing airfields in Saudi Arabia. Although Kirk did not receive from the State Department details about the airfields or air routes desired from the Saudis, he did learn prior to his departure from Cairo that the British minister in Jidda had previously approached the Saudi finance minister concerning the possibility of obtaining overflight rights and airfields in Saudi Arabia. As a result, Kirk raised this subject with the finance minister and was very pleased when the latter assured him that there would be no objection to the flight of American planes over Saudi Arabia or to the establishment of airfields on the Saudi coast.

Upon receiving details from the War Department as to the specific routes and areas that were desired, the State Department on July 7, 1942, alerted Kirk that discussions with the Saudis might begin. Officials in Washington were pessimistic about the likely Saudi response, doubting the utility of approaching Ibn Saud unless the request was accompanied by an offer of substantial assistance and unless the king was assured that his country would be protected from an Axis attack. Both Kirk and Moose were more optimistic, believing that the king would grant permission for overflights of Saudi Arabia and probably also for airfields.

The optimism expressed by Kirk and Moose proved to be well founded. In August 1942 Ibn Saud approved the requests for overflights submitted by the American and British missions in Jidda. This permission was very helpful to the Allies in providing a direct route for their aircraft carrying war materiel via Iran to the Soviet Union. Moreover, the king did not demand an immediate quid pro quo in terms of economic assistance for the facilities he was providing.[5] Ibn Saud's generosity was particularly noteworthy in view of the difficulties facing the Allies at the time, and the widespread speculation that Hitler might launch a military operation to take over the Middle East. The State Department itself shared some of this concern, instructing a senior Army officer who was traveling to the region in July 1942 to look into what measures might be necessary to defend the oil installations in Saudi Arabia (and Bahrain) or to carry out demolition work to deny them to the Axis, should a German seizure appear probable. Interestingly, the United States still accorded the primary responsibility for defending Saudi Arabia to Britain. The State Department notified Kirk on August 28, 1942, that, because of this determination, the War Department would not plan for any American involvement in this area.

As the war continued, however, and as United States military activity grew apace, the Roosevelt administration became increasingly interested in solidifying ties with Saudi Arabia and less disposed to take a secondary position with regard to the British. The first move came in January 1943, when the State Department recommended to Edward R. Stettinius, Jr., the Lend-Lease administrator, that Saudi Arabia be added to the list of countries eligible to receive Lend-Lease aid. The memorandum, signed by Assistant Secretary of State Dean Acheson, noted that the Saudi government had granted the United States overflight rights and that additional privileges would probably not be accorded unless America furnished direct assistance to Saudi Arabia. It added that the proposed aid program should probably be modest and that Ibn Saud's unswerving sympathy for and loyalty to the Allies' cause had been of inestimable value. Stettinius in turn recommended that the president make the necessary finding that defense of Saudi Arabia was vital to that of the United States, and on February 18, 1943, President Roosevelt did so.[6]

In April 1943 Kirk traveled to Saudi Arabia in order to discuss Lend-Lease matters personally with King Ibn Saud. He found the king grateful to receive the assistance. The first shipment, some eighty trucks, arrived shortly thereafter, and almost immediately the number of Saudi aid requests mounted. On April 24, 1943, the American charge learned from his British counterpart that the Saudis were about to ask the United States for arms aid and for gold bullion to compensate for a shortage of currency in the country.

These requests coincided with a growing appreciation in Washington of the importance of American ties with Saudi Arabia. On March 30, 1943, Secretary of State Cordell Hull wrote the president recommending that the status of the charge in Jidda be raised to that of minister and proposing that the incumbent charge, James S. Moose, Jr., be so designated. The secretary stressed that one of the largest oil reserves in the world was located in Saudi Arabia, that the American-owned California Arabian Standard Oil Company held the concession giving it access to the oil reserves, and that in view of the rapid decline of the oil resources in the United States, the War and Navy departments were interested in obtaining reserves in the ground in Saudi Arabia. The president agreed, and on May 19, 1943, Moose assumed the position of minister resident in Jidda.[7]

The newly increased American interest in Saudi Arabia collided with the traditional British position of influence in the area dating to before World War I, which the British government wanted to see increase. When on January 18, 1943, Kirk urged American participation in a proposed package being put together by the British to help provide Saudi Arabia with funds to make up for a shortfall in pilgrims, he noted that American involvement would help counterbalance the increasingly discernible tendency toward British economic entrenchment in the area. He added that the existing system, under which American assistance to Saudi Arabia was channeled through the British, had caused the United States to lose considerable prestige in the eyes of the Saudi Arabians, who had come increasingly to feel that the British were their only friends.

The State Department was quick to act upon Kirk's advice. On February 19, 1943, the day after President Roosevelt signed the finding making Saudi Arabia eligible for Lend-Lease assistance, the Department's adviser on International Economic Affairs, Herbert Feis, called upon the British Treasury representative in Washington. Feis commented that the budget of Saudi Arabia over the past few years had been continuously in the red, and that the British and American governments had both been called upon to make up the deficits. He noted that the advances of the British government to that point exceeded some $20 million and those from American oil companies some $10 million, and the United States government was on the point of extending Lend-Lease assistance on a modest scale to Saudi Arabia. Feis added that American oil companies had large properties in Saudi Arabia and that the United States government had a great interest in the stability and welfare of the Saudi government. He also pointedly remarked that the State Department was interested in learning the details of financial discussions that were reportedly under way between the British and Saudis and might well wish to participate jointly with them in any proposed aid package to be provided Saudi Arabia.[8]

Virtually the same pattern was repeated with regard to the Saudi interest in obtaining American arms. Uncertain as to how Britain and the United States had divided their responsibilities with regard to Saudi Arabia, the Saudis in April 1943 approached the British legation in Jidda for approval to request arms under Lend-Lease from the United States. The British minister straightforwardly informed Kirk of this matter and the latter immediately notified the State Department. The fact that Britain was being asked to serve as the conduit for American assistance left Secretary of State Hull in high dudgeon. On May 25, 1943, he sent a strong note to Admiral William D. Leahy, the president's chief of staff, stating that whereas the United States had agreed at the Casablanca conference in January 1943 that military equipment for Turkey would be forwarded through British channels, this agreement did not extend to other areas of the Middle East. The secretary was particularly concerned that the

British government had advised the Saudis to make their request for American arms via the Saudi legation in London or the British legation in Jidda. Hull noted that if unchallenged by the United States, this procedure would mean that the Saudi government, whose economic interests were closely related to those of the United States by virtue of the oil concession granted the California Arabian Standard oil Company, could secure American military equipment only through the medium of the British authorities. The secretary concluded by pointing out that he was aware of no agreement under which the United States had agreed to this procedure and that it would be highly damaging to American prestige throughout the Arab world and prejudicial to vital American economic interests to let this become established policy.

Admiral Leahy at once confirmed to Hull that he knew of no understandings committing the United States to work through the British, other than in Turkey. He added that the American Joint Chiefs of Staff agreed with Hull's proposal to inform the British government that there was no need for Saudi arms requests to be forwarded via British channels. The State Department accordingly sent word of the United States policy to the embassy in London and to the American legations in Jidda, Cairo, Baghdad, and Tehran on June 7, 1943.

If the British had had any ulterior motives, they gracefully yielded to the United States on the matter. On July 8, 1943, the Foreign Office told the American embassy in London that it had never been the intention of the British to suggest that Ibn Saud was precluded from approaching the United States directly for aid. The proposal that he submit his request via the British had been in conformity with an unofficial *modus operandi* under which requests for war supplies from countries were forwarded either through Washington or London to prevent the confusion that might arise if a country submitted simultaneous requests for arms to both capitals. The Foreign Office added that the British had strictly adhered to this procedure in countries in the United States' sphere of strategic responsibility, as defined by the Combined British and American Joint Chiefs of Staff.[9]

Pursuant to his instructions, Moose informed the British minister in Jidda and appropriate Saudi officials that the requests for arms assistance should be directly presented to the United States, and these were not slow in coming. On July 9, 1943, the Saudi acting foreign minister delivered to the legation a list of military aid desired under Lend-Lease, to include rifles, ammunition, tanks, antiaircraft guns, and airplanes, as well as American advisers to instruct in the use of the equipment. The acting foreign minister indicated that the Saudi government could use virtually any quantity of material available, and that its goal was to equip a force of 100,000 men.[10]

The United States also now became involved in providing financial assistance to the Saudi government. To counter a shortage of gold in Saudi Arabia and a lack of confidence in Saudi paper currency, the British had previously provided coinage as part of their financial support.

Having indicated its interest in participating jointly with the British in providing financial aid to Saudi Arabia, the State Department began to follow closely the state of the Saudi currency scene. On July 10, 1943, in a message to the American minister in Jidda, the Department noted that it was endeavoring to find a means of financing the purchase of silver and minting silver coins needed by Saudi Arabia.

The administrative procedures required in Washington between the time aid was requested and when it could be approved and shipped were extremely cumbersome, so that considerable delay ensued before the assistance was actually delivered. With regard to the financial help, the Treasury Department determined as an initial step to send its own representative, John W. Gunter, to look into conditions in Saudi Arabia. His mission was both to ensure that silver furnished would be returned in kind, a requirement under the Lend-Lease legislation, and to develop a long-range program of assisting the Saudi government to establish a sound and working fiscal system. Gunter visited Jidda in August 1943 and after conversations with Saudi officials recommended that the silver be provided to Saudi Arabia under Lend-Lease. Additional delays resulted as a result of the need to determine which Saudi official's signature would be acceptable on the commitment to eventually return the silver. For protocol reasons the king was unwilling to do so unless President Roosevelt also signed the agreement. After some discussion, the matter was solved and an adviser to the king signed the necessary documents on October 3, 1943, providing some $2 million in silver to the Saudis to be used for coinage.

The path for the requested military assistance also was not without obstacles. After reviewing the list of equipment that Saudi Arabia wanted the United States to supply, the British Foreign Office in August 1943 demurred. In a note to the American embassy in London, the British Foreign Office stated that it was clearly desirable that Ibn Saud possess sufficient arms and military equipment to enable him to maintain order among his tribesmen and throughout his territories. At the same time, however, the British pointed out that for many years they had devoted considerable effort to controlling the traffic in arms in the region. The Foreign Office added that undue quantities of arms in the hands of the Saudis would probably lead to their being smuggled there and increase instability in the Middle East, and that the Saudi monarchy was not in a position to pay for any of the requested material. For these reasons, the Foreign Office urged that the amount of arms provided Saudi Arabia be limited to fifty light reconnaissance cars, 500 light machine guns, and 10,000 rifles and ammunition.[11]

The British had already made plans to deliver much of this equipment to Saudi Arabia on the assumption that these quantities met the latter's valid needs, but agreed to a State Department request to delay delivery until the United States could complete a study as to what arms Saudi Arabia should have and the quantities that could be made available. On

September 20, 1943, the State Department informed Kirk in Cairo that the War Department was giving consideration to the Saudi Arabian government's request for Lend-Lease military equipment but that the information furnished by the Saudi authorities was insufficient to permit proper plans. Accordingly Major General Ralph Royce, Commanding Officer of the United States Forces in the Middle East, headquartered in Cairo, sent a staff officer to Jidda to discuss military assistance to Saudi Arabia in September 1943 and followed this up with a survey mission there himself in December. Based on this review, the State Department in January 1944 informed the British that it agreed to their suggestion that military supplies furnished Saudi Arabia be limited to the types and quantities necessary to maintain law and order in that country, and that the assistance should be provided in equal measure by America and Britain. In March 1944 some 1,600 rifles and 350,000 rounds of ammunition arrived at the American legation in Jidda to be turned over to the Saudis, followed in April 1944 by a twelve-man American military training mission headed by Colonel Garret B. Shomber. This humble beginning marked the start of a long-term association between the United States and Saudi Arabia in the field of military cooperation and one that came to affect significantly the bilateral relations between the two nations. Meanwhile, as the United States moved to strengthen ties with Saudi Arabia, it also gave increased attention to that nation's vast oil reserves.

ENDNOTES

1. *Foreign Relations, 1941,* Washington, D.C., 1959, Vol. III, pp. 624-627.

2. *Ibid.,* pp. 642-649.

3. *Ibid.,* pp. 648-659.

4. *Foreign Relations, 1942,* Washington, D.C., 1963, Vol. IV, pp. 559-563.

5. *Ibid.,* pp. 566-575.

6. *Foreign Relations, 1943,* Washington, D.C., 1964, Vol. IV, p. 859.

7. *Ibid.,* p. 832.

8. *Ibid.,* pp. 856-860.

9. *Ibid.,* pp. 1-5.

10. *Ibid.,* pp. 873-874.

11. *Ibid.,* pp. 885-886.

CHAPTER 4
The Importance of Saudi Oil

Benson Lee Grayson

Although the American oil concession in Saudi Arabia dated back to 1933, the greatly expanded consumption of oil in World War II caused the United States to give increased priority to assuring a sufficient supply. On June 8, 1943, Admiral Leahy, on behalf of the American Joint Chiefs of Staff, addressed a memorandum to President Roosevelt warning that America had an insufficient supply of domestic crude oil production to meet the requirements of the armed forces and essential civilian needs. In the interests of national security he urged that steps be taken immediately to ensure continued control of enough oil reserves to meet America's needs and recommended that the government Reconstruction and Finance Corporation organize a corporation for the purpose of acquiring foreign petroleum reserves. The president was persuaded of the importance of the problem and directed Leahy to meet personally with Secretary of State Hull to make arrangements for the United States government to obtain sufficient oil reserves by acquiring an interest in the Saudi oil fields. Roosevelt, influenced by his service in the Navy Department, suggested that the United States obtain from the Saudi government an oil concession that would be similar in purpose to the naval oil fuel reserves in America, which the United States could tap when necessary and pay the Saudi government the usual royalty for the oil as it was taken.

The secretary of state recognized the importance of petroleum matters upon the whole fabric of American foreign policy and was unwilling to risk bureaucratic controversy by allocating to himself complete jurisdiction in the matter. He instead suggested that the ultimate decision be made by the president based upon the findings of a committee including representatives from the State, War, Navy, and Interior departments and from the Office of War Mobilization. As a result, the suggested meetings were held in mid-June 1943, presided over by James F. Byrnes, former justice of the Supreme Court and future secretary of state, who was then serving as director of the Office of War Mobilization. The committee report, concurred in by all the members, was sent to the president on June 25, 1943. It recommended that a new corporation to acquire foreign oil reserves be established prior to July 1, 1943, and that the corporation immediately initiate steps to acquire an interest in the highly important Saudi Arabian oil fields. The report left to the recommendation of Justice Byrnes such details as the directorate and control of the corporation, the type of interest or ownership in the Saudi oil reserves, and the method of paying for them. Among the thorny questions thus deferred for future decision were whether the new government corporation would take over any of the oil fields in the concession operated by the California Arabian Standard Oil Company, acquire some or all of the stock in that company, and whether the company or its two parents, the Standard Oil Company of California and the Texas Corporation, would have any role in operating the government company.[1]

The proposed company, named the Petroleum Reserve Corporation, was established as planned on June 30, 1943. The State Department asked the American legation in Jidda to furnish detail on the status of the California Arabian Standard Oil Company operations to help frame United States policy. In retrospect, it is clear that the Roosevelt administration would have had considerable difficulty in implementing its plans to acquire a share of the Arabian oil fields without significant company participation. Indeed, when the Army and Navy concluded in July 1943 that the American government should erect an oil refinery in Saudi Arabia to help the military effort in the Southwest Pacific, the Petroleum Reserves Corporation quickly brought the California Arabian Standard Oil Company into the picture, authorizing it to construct the refinery.

In any event, the American minister in Cairo, Alexander Kirk, weighed in with his views and recommendations against excluding the company. In a message addressed to Secretary Hull on July 27, 1943, Kirk stated that throughout his service as minister to Saudi Arabia he had been impressed by the high standards maintained by the California Arabian Standard Oil Company in all its activities and by the regard with which King Ibn Saud viewed the company. Not only was it held in esteem for its oil operations, but also for its involvement in establishing schools, planning irrigation projects, and otherwise contributing to the development of the country. Kirk warned that the United States government lacked personnel with the specialized business experience to deal with conditions in Saudi Arabia. Further, overt government involvement in the oil concessions would raise fears in the mind of the king as to Washington's ulterior political motives and the United States would come to be regarded with the same suspicion the Saudis accorded Britain and other European nations.[2]

Moreover, the representatives of the Petroleum Reserves Corporation found the officials of the Standard Oil Company of California and Texas Corporation, with whom they discussed a possible government takeover of some of the oil company operations and properties in Saudi Arabia, less than helpful. This was a logical reaction stemming from the companies' reluctance to cede the potentially hugely profitable oil fields. In a report to the secretary of state on December 14, 1943, the political adviser of the Department noted that government negotiations with the private firms had gone through three stages: the first, in which the Petroleum Reserves Corporation had tried successively to take over the entire holdings of the California Arabian Standard in Saudi Arabia; the next, the negotiations for majority control; and finally, the agreement for one-third of the stock, with the private firms each retaining one-third. While continuing to believe that the interests of the United States required the participation of the government in the protection of the American oil reserves, the directors of the Petroleum Reserves Corporation were forced to conclude that the companies' representatives had been unable or unwilling to appreciate the need for the involvement of the United States government.

Another factor complicating a possible government role in the Saudi oil fields stemmed from press reports of Washington's interests in acquiring a share of the Saudi Reserves. On October 21, 1943, the *Wall Street Journal* carried a front-page article stating that the Petroleum Reserves Corporation had held negotiations with the California Arabian Standard Oil Company to acquire the company's holdings in Saudi Arabia. Realizing that the news of the American government's objective could not long be kept from the Saudis, if in fact they were not already aware of it, the State Department in November 1943 instructed the American minister in Jidda to brief the king. The minister informed Ibn Saud that the United States planned to build a large refinery in the Middle East, that discussions were under way with the California Arabian Standard Oil Company with a view to possibly locating the refinery in Saudi Arabia, and that Washington was talking with the firm about securing a part interest in it to protect the government's interests. Ironically, when this information was communicated to Ibn Saud he remarked that he had already learned of it from the general manager of the California Arabian Standard Oil Company and that he regarded American government participation as perfectly natural and not something to be opposed.[3]

If Ibn Saud was not afraid of direct Washington participation in the Saudi oil fields, the State Department was coming to doubt the wisdom of this policy. In addition to the factors already cited, the Department was concerned over the impact this would have on Britain, possibly leading that country to provide greater support for British oil interests in the Middle East and thus causing long-term harm to the future operations of American oil companies. On November 13, 1943, Secretary Hull informed Secretary of the Interior Harold I. Ickes, in the latter's capacity as president of the Petroleum Reserves Corporation, that the State Department had learned that influence would be brought to bear upon King Ibn Saud for the purpose of undermining his confidence in the American interest in Saudi oil resources. Hull further feared that the British financial support that the king had been obliged by his country's weakened economy to obtain gave Great Britain an opportunity to secure an interest in the Saudi Arabian oil at the expense of the United States companies. Noting that Saudi oil was one of the world's greatest prizes and that it would be extremely short-sighted to take any steps that would tend to discredit the American interest, Hull recommended that steps be taken to end the appearance of controversy between the administration and the American companies, even if this required giving up the plan to secure a government share in the oil reserves. At the same time, the State Department proposed that high-level discussions be held with the British government to work out a common understanding on petroleum matters.

On December 2, 1943, the secretary of state asked the British ambassador in Washington to transmit to London an invitation for the two governments to discuss petroleum problems of mutual interest. Informing President Roosevelt of the invitation, Hull stressed the need for avoiding a dispute with London over oil, pointing out that the Middle East oil reserves could not be adequately developed unless the United States and British governments reached an agreement calling for close cooperation.

Meanwhile, as the United States first moved toward acquiring a government share in the Saudi oil fields and then retreated in favor of leaving the predominant role to the American oil companies and of working in close association with the British, another factor intruded on the scene. The issue was not a new one and indeed is still a major factor in Saudi Arabian-American relations today. It involved the United States interest in establishing a Jewish homeland in what was then Palestine and the Saudi backing for Arab groups in Palestine who opposed this development.

As noted previously, Ibn Saud had expressed his belief in a letter to President Roosevelt in December 1938 that the United States appeared to be taking a position sympathetic to the Zionist cause. This fear was never far from the king's mind. He referred to it again in April 1943, when Kirk traveled from Cairo to Jidda to work out with the Saudis arrangements for American Lend-Lease assistance. On the day of the minister's departure, the king sent for him and declared that there was a matter that he desired to discuss in the strictest confidence. Indicating that he wanted to have the minister transmit his message to the president, the king stated that the Palestine situation was of more concern to him than to any other Arab leader and that the Jews had been hostile to the Arabs from the time of the Prophet Mohammed to the present. As the leading Arab and Moslem, the king believed he had a special interest in developments in Palestine where, because of their vast wealth and influence in Britain and the United States, Jews were steadily encroaching on the Arabs. Ibn Saud warned that if this trend were allowed to continue, the Jewish-Arab conflict would become more acute and might affect the Allied war effort.[4]

Not content with his conversation with Kirk, the king on April 30, 1943, sent a letter to President Roosevelt, stressing his concern over the Palestine situation. He asserted that the Zionists were taking advantage of the conditions brought about by the war to gain the assistance of the Allies to exterminate the peaceful Arabs settled in Palestine. Ibn Saud went on to urge that the president assist in stopping the flow of Jewish migration. The king noted that Palestine was a small area, and that the percentage of Jews in the population had risen from seven percent after World War I to 29 percent. He suggested that the Jewish problem could be solved by each of the Allied countries permitting a share of the Jews to settle in their territory.

Commenting on Ibn Saud's interest in Palestine, the American legation in Jidda underscored the seriousness of the king's warning. It advised the State Department on May 6, 1943, that in the past there had been three great bases for Ibn Saud's policies: first, his religion; second, his Arabism; and third, his friendship with the British government. Of the three, the first had always been dominant and in the event of any conflict with the British, the religious motif would undoubtedly prevail. Aside from the king's religious convictions, which would prevent him from ever agreeing to Palestine becoming a Jewish state, the legation declared that practical considerations of Ibn Saud's position in his own country would bar acceptance of any such plan because any indication that he was willing to consider this would weaken or destroy his prestige.[5]

Faced with the adamant position of the king and the countervailing domestic political pressures in the United States, President Roosevelt could respond to Ibn Saud's letter only in general terms and hope that he could avoid irritating either the Arabs or the Jews. A warm response was drafted by the State Department, approved by the president and transmitted to the Saudis on June 2, 1943. In it Roosevelt expressed his thanks for the king's communication, stated America's hope that the Arabs and Jews could together reach a friendly agreement on the matters affecting Palestine, and declared that the United States opposed any change in the basic situation in Palestine undertaken without full consultation with both Arabs and Jews.

At the same time, as the formal American reply to the king's letter, the United States also took steps to attempt to establish an informal dialogue with the Saudis to relieve the tension and possibly solve the Palestine situation. In July 1943, the president sent a special emissary, Lieutenant Colonel Harold B. Hoskins, to learn informally from the king his views with regard to Palestine. An Army officer and Arabic linguist, Colonel Hoskins had earlier made a three-and-one-half-month survey trip to the Near East and North Africa for the State Department in 1943. After a week of frank and lengthy discussions with Hoskins, Ibn Saud categorically rejected President Roosevelt's suggestion that he meet with a representative of the Jewish Agency to discuss a possible solution to the Palestine problem.

In September 1943, Colonel Hoskins met personally with the president to brief him on the results of his trip. At the meeting, Roosevelt indicated his own views as to a possible compromise on Palestine. The president suggested that Palestine be transformed into a real Holy Land for the Christians, Moslems, and Jews, with a representative of each religion serving as one of the three responsible trustees. Hoskins also found Roosevelt very interested in learning his impression of Ibn Saud. The president was particularly impressed by the fact that the king had acquired a wide grasp of world affairs, in part through his radio monitoring service, which kept him informed several times a day of what was being reported on the radio in various Axis and Allied countries.[6]

The president's questioning of Hoskins concerning Ibn Saud and other members of the Saudi royal family was linked to the pending state visit to the United States of two of the king's sons: Amir Faisal, the foreign minister, and Amir Khalid.

This was an important event in Saudi-American relations because it marked the first time such high-level Saudi dignitaries were to visit America and because both princes were subsequently to occupy the Saudi throne. Faisal ruled from 1964 until his assassination in 1975, and Khalid after that date. The initial suggestion for a royal visit was made by the Saudis during a trip by Kirk to Saudi Arabia in 1942, when they informed him that Crown Prince Saud wished to visit the United States after the end of World War II. In July 1943, as part of the campaign to strengthen ties with Jidda, the State Department sent a message from President Roosevelt inviting the king or some other member of the royal family to make such a visit. Ibn Saud accepted, subsequently informing the American legation that the crown prince could not then leave the country because of the press of state business, but that Faisal and Khalid would go in his stead.

The two princes arrived in the United States in October 1943, holding discussions with senior State Department officials and being received by President Roosevelt during their stay. The visit generally went well, with the administration happily accepting a Saudi request that aid requests be made directly to the American legation in Jidda. Amir Faisal indicated that his father would approve any proposals President Roosevelt might forward concerning a role by the American government in the Saudi oil fields when the State Department raised the subject as a contingency measure. The importance that the Saudis attached to maintaining close relations with the United States was apparent in the comments made by the two princes. In a meeting with undersecretary and acting secretary of state Edward R. Stettinius, Jr., on November 1, 1943, Faisal stressed that Ibn Saud wanted to be fully informed as to the objectives of American policy in the Middle East because he did not want to take any actions that might be at variance with it.

Naturally the Saudis had their own axe to grind. Faisal referred to reports that the Hashemite family, the former rulers of the Hejaz whom Ibn Saud had vanquished, were working for a union of Palestine, Iraq, and Syria in order to surround Saudi Arabia and regain control of it. Because Hashemite rulers reigned in both Transjordan (present-day Jordan) and Iraq, this was not a prospect the Saudis could easily dismiss. The American reply was probably not entirely satisfactory to Faisal. Although the United States had no interest in making dynastic alliances against Ibn Saud or anyone else, neither would the United States adopt a less friendly attitude toward the governments of Transjordan and Iraq, both of which were supported by Great Britain. The State Department officials made clear that American policy toward the Middle East was based upon the high-sounding principle, agreed to by President Roosevelt and British Prime Minister Winston Churchill in the Atlantic Charter Declaration of August 1942, that every nation was entitled to a government of its own choosing.[7]

If, as explained to the two Saudi princes, American policy toward Saudi Arabia and the rest of the Middle East was both simple and idealistic, it was not without its more pragmatic features. Among the complicating factors were the still unsolved dispute between the American oil companies and the Petroleum Reserves Corporation over their respective roles in Saudi oil, differences between various elements of the American government over what United States oil policy should be, and the potential rivalry between the British and American governments and oil companies in the Middle East. All of these elements came into play as 1944 began.

On December 27, 1943, the president of the California Arabian Standard Oil Company wrote to the State Department to inform it that, anticipating greatly increased Saudi oil production after the war, the company planned to build a large pipeline to transport petroleum from Saudi Arabia to a refinery to be constructed on the Mediterranean. Although the company possessed the necessary rights within Saudi Arabia, it wanted the department's views and possible assistance in negotiating with other countries through which the pipeline might pass, including Transjordan, Palestine, and possibly Egypt. The State Department response was quite warm. Charles B. Rayner, the acting petroleum adviser, informed the company on January 7, 1944, that the department would in principle look favorably upon the project and was prepared to assist in every appropriate way to secure the necessary rights and safeguards for construction of the pipeline.

Although the State Department tended to be sympathetic to the role of the American oil companies in Saudi Arabia and the Middle East in general, the Department of the Interior, in the person of Secretary Harold Ickes, was more critical. As president of the Petroleum Reserves Corporation, he naturally favored a decisive voice for that entity. Coincidental with the pipeline matter, Secretary of State Hull on January 5, 1944, sent a letter to Ickes requesting that the Petroleum Reserves Corporation hold in abeyance all negotiations with the American oil companies concerning their oil reserves until the discussions planned with the British on petroleum matters were concluded. The secretary of the interior, however, was cool to this proposal, feeling that it contravened the instructions to the Petroleum Reserves Corporation that had been concurred by the State Department and approved by President Roosevelt. In a written response, Ickes told Hull that he could not join in recommending that the plans for the Petroleum Reserves Corporation be abandoned. The interior secretary felt this would be a grave error that would prejudice America's position with regard to the Persian Gulf oil reserves for generations to come. He added that King Ibn Saud had indicated he would welcome American government participation in the Arabian American Oil Company (Aramco), as the California Arabian Standard Oil Company was renamed. Finally, Ickes believed that London could hardly object to the United States government acquiring an interest in the companies or the oil reserves, because the British government itself possessed such interest and influence over the British companies operating in the Persian Gulf area.[8]

Informed of the impasse between his two Cabinet members, President Roosevelt reacted with annoyance that they had not been able to reach agreement without involving him in the dispute. On January 10, 1944, he returned it to them to solve, indicating his general support for Ickes' position that government discussions with the American companies not be deferred. The secretary of the interior's victory was only temporary, however. By February 1944, when he announced the signing of a contract with Aramco for construction of a pipeline from Saudi Arabia to the Mediterranean, he was obliged to add in the official press release that the Petroleum Reserves Corporation did not propose to compete with the private oil industry of the United States.

Ickes' retreat was a result, in part, of the successful pressure mounted by the American oil industry, which did not wish to see the government assume an operating role. It was also a result of the feeling in Congress that such an expansion of government activity into what was normally handled by the private sector would be unwise. Indeed, although the new pipeline agreement was relatively favorable to the American oil companies in Arabia, giving them the benefit of a pipeline to be built at government expense but with repayment guaranteed by the companies, it too was subjected to such intense criticism in the United States that it was never implemented.

Meanwhile, the State Department intensified its cooperation with the American oil companies. On February 2, 1944, Secretary Hull met with the heads of the American oil firms operating abroad and with the president of the American Petroleum Institute to advise them of the forthcoming discussions with the British on oil matters and to solicit their views. He took the occasion to enunciate as United States government policy the position that if any country granted to foreigners rights concerning the exploration or development of petroleum resources, the nationals of the United States should be accorded equal opportunity to obtain such rights. In a message on February 17, 1944, informing several American diplomatic missions of the new policy guidelines, the State Department instructed its representatives to render all appropriate assistance to the representatives of American oil companies who might be seeking petroleum concessions.

The preeminence of the State Department in framing American policy with regard to international oil matters and the department's close cooperation with American international oil companies meant that the views emanating from these two quarters would have a significant effect upon United States policy toward Saudi Arabia. The official encouragement given by Secretary Hull to American oil companies operating abroad had particular emphasis in the Middle East. On February 15, 1944, President Roosevelt established a Cabinet committee to prepare for the petroleum discussions with the British headed by Secretary Hull and with Secretary Ickes as vice chairman. A State Department paper on the objectives of United States foreign petroleum policy prepared as part of the preparations for the meeting with the British stressed that emphasis should be given to conserving the petroleum reserves of the Western hemisphere in order to assure the adequacy of strategically available reserves. As a corollary to this policy, exports of oil from the Western hemisphere to the Eastern hemisphere were to be curtailed as much as possible and American firms urged to expand their development of oil in the Eastern hemisphere. The paper noted that insofar as development of Eastern hemisphere oil was delayed by existing conflicts between the United States and Great Britain, a close understanding with the British was desirable in order to implement the basic American policy.[9]

The meeting with the British to discuss cooperation in the Middle East on oil and other matters took place in London from April 7 through 29, 1944, with the American delegation headed by Undersecretary of State Stettinius. The two sides reached agreement with regard to the division of responsibilities and influence in Saudi Arabia. Whereas in Britain it was political and strategic interests in that country were recognized as paramount, the United States considered its oil interests there to be of primary importance. The British categorically disclaimed any intention to undermine or prejudice American oil rights in Saudi Arabia, and agreed that the larger financial and supply problems of that country should be dealt with as far as possible on a joint basis in consultation between the two governments.[10] Although the American delegation returned from the talks relatively pleased with the outcome, their satisfaction was premature. A period of nasty rivalry between the United States and Britain was about to begin.

The British had already made plans to deliver much of this equipment to Saudi Arabia on the assumption that these quantities met the latter's valid needs, but agreed to a State Department request to delay delivery until the United States could complete a study as to what arms Saudi Arabia should have and the quantities that could be made available. On September 20, 1943, the State Department informed Kirk in Cairo that the War Department was giving consideration to the Saudi Arabian government's request for Lend-Lease military equipment but that the information furnished by the Saudi authorities was insufficient to permit proper plans. Accordingly Major General Ralph Royce, commanding officer of the United States Forces in the Middle East, headquartered in Cairo, sent a staff officer to Jidda to discuss military assistance to Saudi Arabia in September 1943 and followed this up with a survey mission there himself in December. Based on this review, the State Department in January 1944 informed the British that it agreed to their suggestion that military supplies furnished Saudi Arabia be limited to the types and quantities necessary to maintain law and order in that country, and that the assistance should be provided in equal measure by America and Britain. In March 1944 some 1,600 rifles and 350,000 rounds of ammunition arrived at the American legation in Jidda to be turned over to the Saudis, followed in April 1944 by a twelve-man American military training mission headed by Colonel Garret B. Shomber. This humble beginning marked the start of a long-term association between the United States and Saudi Arabia in the field of military cooperation and one that came to affect significantly the bilateral relations between the two nations. Meanwhile, as the United States moved to strengthen ties with Saudi Arabia, it also gave increased attention to that nation's vast oil reserves.

ENDNOTES

1. *Foreign Relations, 1943,* Washington, D.C., 1964, Vol. IV, pp. 921-930.

2. *Ibid.,* pp. 935-937.

3. *Ibid.,* pp. 941-950.

4. *Ibid.,* pp. 768-771.

5. *Ibid.,* pp. 780-781.

6. *Ibid.,* pp. 811-814.

7. *Ibid.,* pp. 841-847.

8. *Foreign Relations, 1944,* Washington, D.C., 1965, Vol. V, pp. 12-15.

9. *Ibid.,* pp. 23-28.

10. *Foreign Relations, 1944,* Washington, D.C., 1965, Vol. III, pp. 29-30.

CHAPTER 5
Rivalry with the British

Benson Lee Grayson

The understanding reached by the United States and British conferees in April 1944 concerning the relative priority of interests in Saudi Arabia might have worked out well in an ideal world. In practice, however, the understanding was subject to such great pressure from the force of events and open to such wide diversity of interpretation that it was collapsing even at the moment of its inception.

The first area of contention came in the matter of the economic assistance to be furnished Saudi Arabia. On January 25, 1944, the American minister in Jidda cabled the State Department that the Saudi acting minister for foreign affairs had that day notified him that the Saudi government was completely out of funds and that the king had inquired when additional currency minted out of the American Lend-Lease silver would arrive. More depressing news on the state of the Saudi economy reached Washington on February 26, 1944, when the legation in Jidda reported that the king was disturbed over the position of Saudi Arabia with regard to the adequacy of the food supply, the distribution of food and other essential goods from ports to the interior and over government finances. The minister, Moose, implied that something underhanded might be going on between the Saudis and the British, that the British minister in Jidda had offered to keep the American legation informed as to his conversations with the king and had then failed to do so, and that the American legation was having difficulty in obtaining reliable information concerning the exact status of the economic situation in the country.[1]

Alarmed by these tidings, Washington responded in energetic fashion. On April 3, 1944, Secretary Hull recommended to President Roosevelt that the United States extend additional economic assistance to Saudi Arabia in order to safeguard adequately the American national interest in the petroleum resources of that country. The secretary summarized for the president recent disturbing developments: the fact that in recent years the Saudi government had relied principally upon British subsidies to meet its deficits arising from inadequate sources of revenue, that in 1944 London planned to subsidize Saudi Arabia by providing about $12 million to purchase foodstuffs and textiles from British sources (a sum roughly six times greater than the value of Lend-Lease projected by the American government for Jidda in the same year), and that the British minister in Saudi Arabia had apparently persuaded King Ibn Saud to remove from office key Saudi officials known to be friendly to the United States and to agree to appoint a British economic adviser and possibly a British petroleum adviser. Hull warned that if Saudi Arabia were permitted to lean too heavily upon the British, there was a clear danger that London would request a quid pro quo in oil. He therefore advised Roosevelt that the United States should share the subsidy equally with the British and proposed recommending to the Saudis that they establish a central bank under purely American auspices. If implemented, this would have given Washington a wide measure of influence over the Saudi economy.

President Roosevelt gave his complete approval to the recommendations submitted by Hull. In notifying the American legation in Jidda of this development on April 13, 1944, the State Department requested that it obtain accurate factual information on the financial and economic needs of Saudi Arabia to enable Washington to formulate concrete plans for the extension of aid to that country. Interestingly, while the State Department instruction noted that plans for joint American-British assistance would have to be discussed with London, the tone of the message indicated that the United States would not accept second place to the British in Saudi Arabia.[2]

The State Department's suspicions were further inflamed in mid-April 1944 when a Foreign Office official told a member of the Stettinius mission in London that the British government, at the request of King Ibn Saud, was contemplating furnishing the Saudi Arabian government with a financial adviser and military advisers to train and establish an army on modern lines. To the United States, this seemed a clear slap in the face, because an American military mission had that month arrived in Saudi Arabia for the same purpose. Aware of this, the Foreign Office official explained that Ibn Saud wanted the British mission to consist entirely of Sunni Moslems, because their religious views were the nearest to those of the Saudi royal family. Additionally, as Moslems they could reside in Mecca, which the American military mission could not. Similarly, the British were seeking an appropriate financial adviser among their Moslem personnel in India. Confirmation of this threat to American interests in Saudi Arabia, for such it was received in Washington, came from the American legation in Jidda, which reported on April 15, 1944, that it had received virtually the same information from the British minister in Jidda. The latter added to the American feeling of resentment by observing that the British mission would in no way conflict with the American military mission, because that mission would stay on only a few months to teach the Saudis the use of the newly supplied American weapons and would then retire, leaving the British mission to train and organize the Saudi forces. Finally, the British minister observed, it really would be advantageous to the

United States to have a British military mission in Saudi Arabia because of the added security it would afford to the Saudi oil fields, which, he noted, were very large and important.

In retrospect, the British were probably trying to obtain a position of first among equals with regard to the United States in Saudi Arabia but were not guilty of gross deception. Much of the confusion appears to have stemmed from the fact that Ibn Saud was unhappy over the extent of the aid he was receiving from the British and Americans and fearful that the latter and possibly both might desert him when they no longer needed Saudi friendship after the war. Moreover, rather than supplant the American financial assistance to Jidda, London was at least equally interested in easing its burden by reducing the level of the aid furnished Saudi Arabia. However, each of the three participants in the equation, the Americans, British, and Saudis, was basing its actions upon incomplete and frequently inaccurate information of the others' intentions. Not surprisingly, the confusion continued.

On April 18, 1944, the American legation in Jidda reported that no agreement had yet been reached on the extent or kind of aid to be given by the British government to Saudi Arabia. Ibn Saud had written to the British minister asking for a written statement of what London was prepared to provide, noting that if the intended aid were not sufficient, his country would look to other sources, including Aramco. The American minister, Moose, warned the State Department that if the British persisted in their present policy of drastic economy with regard to aid to Saudi Arabia, the harmful political effects might well outweigh the beneficial economic ones.

On the same day Moose was dispatching his warning to the State Department, the latter was sending him instructions on steps to take to prevent the American presence in Saudi Arabia from being eclipsed by the British. He was encouraged to make frequent trips to Riyadh, the capital, in order to keep in close touch with the king. The department also instructed Moose to suggest to Ibn Saud that Colonel William A. Eddy, former president of Hobart and William Smith College and an Arabic scholar then serving as a special assistant to Moose, after having been detailed by the United States Marine Corps for duty with the State Department, serve the king as financial and economic adviser, as well as military adviser.

At this juncture, the American minister to Egypt and former minister to Saudi Arabia, Alexander Kirk, weighed in with his comments concerning the situation in Saudi Arabia. Citing his experiences in Jidda, Kirk volunteered to the department on April 25, 1944, that he feared Saudi Arabia was rapidly becoming an active battleground between the differing foreign policies of Great Britain and the United States. The former, he suggested, traditionally aimed at making countries in which it had an interest dependent in perpetuity upon London, whereas America sought to help backward countries progress to the point of reaching real independence. Kirk warned that the competition between the two philosophies was injuring

Western prestige in Jidda and urged that Washington and London thrash out a settlement that could be communicated to their respective missions in Saudi Arabia and that would lead to their activities there being conducted in a spirit of cooperation rather than of competition.[3]

Unlike the American ministers in Egypt and Saudi Arabia, the American ambassador in London was more disposed to give the British the benefit of the doubt. On April 27, 1944, Ambassador Winant reported with pleasure that the talks between the British and the Stettinius mission had led to increasingly close American-British cooperation. In this context, he transmitted a proposal from the Foreign Office that, subject to Ibn Saud's consent, a joint Anglo-American military mission to Saudi Arabia be constituted, to be headed by an "Anglo-Saxon British officer" with Arabian training and experience, with the remainder of the British contingent consisting of Sunni Moslem Indian officers.

Meanwhile, pursuant to his instructions to obtain data on the Saudi economic situation, the American minister in Jidda met on April 23 and April 24, 1944, with Ibn Saud. Informed that President Roosevelt had approved a policy of sharing subsidization of Saudi Arabia equally with the British, the king expressed his satisfaction and promised that his officials would provide the legation with the requested information. At the same time, the king indicated his preference for closer ties with the United States than with the British, a factor that was to have an important impact upon Saudi-American relations in the years to come. He stated that the British would continue to be his friends because of his gratitude over their past aid and because of his fear that they could relax the restraint they were imposing on his enemies, such as the Hashemite dynasties in Transjordan and Iraq. He declared, however, that London's current policies toward Saudi Arabia would ruin his country. Ibn Saud declared that his people were sorely tried by the war-time shortage of consumer goods and by the progressive desiccation of the limited amount of arable land, and that he would be blamed by his people if the financial crisis required him to reduce government expenditure. For this reason, the king stressed, he would very much welcome additional American aid. He added significantly that one day it might be necessary to look to the United States to meet all his country's requirements.[4]

The king's comments struck a warm note with Moose, who as minister in Jidda had to bear the brunt of dealing with British officials, who were more eager to secure a position of preeminence in Saudi Arabia than was the Foreign Office. In a report to the State Department on April 30, 1944, after his meetings with Ibn Saud, Moose warned that the achievement of equality with the British in aid to Saudi Arabia would help, but alone would not assure the protection of American interests. He suggested that the recent activities of the British minister in Jidda and the latter's efforts to obtain a British military mission and financial adviser looked remarkably like an attempt to establish the primacy of British influence in the country. Moose further urged that the United States could adequately protect its interests only if it was ready if necessary to take over the whole problem of providing Saudi Arabia with financial and other assistance until Saudi Arabian oil royalties substantially increased. With the assurance of American help, Moose believed, the king would be able to resist British pressures. Without it, he would be vulnerable.

The State Department, recognizing the widespread cooperation around the world between the United States and Britain, was willing to compromise with London concerning the situation in Saudi Arabia. At the same time, it was not prepared to yield preeminence there to the British. In a cable to the American embassy in London on May 1, 1944, the State Department, with the concurrence of the War Department, gave its approval to the British proposal for a British officer to head a joint American-British military mission to Jidda. This was contingent, however, on London agreeing to an American being named to head any economic or financial mission sent to Saudi Arabia.

Unfortunately, the differences between London and Washington on Saudi Arabia could not so easily be solved. On June 3, 1944, the American legation in Cairo, where technical discussions with the British were under way concerning the level and nature of the bilateral assistance to be furnished Saudi Arabia, informed the State Department that the two sides had been unable to reach agreement because of British determination to effect a drastic reduction not only of the British subsidy but also of all Saudi expenditures. The legation added that the British representatives seemed to consider Saudi stability as of secondary importance, and that, coupled with other projects encouraged by the British minister in Jidda, suggested that he hoped to establish and exercise effective control over the Saudi government.[5]

As though the comments from the legations in Jidda and Cairo were not enough, further disquieting news reached the State Department from the American embassy in London. On June 9, 1944, Ambassador Winant reported receipt of a note from the Foreign Office responding to the compromise proposal. It began by suggesting that Ibn Saud might refuse to accept any Christian officers at all on the proposed American-British military mission, so that if one consisting of only Moslem officers were not acceptable to the United States, then the whole idea might have to be dropped. Concerning the proposed economic or financial adviser, whom the State Department had stated should be an American, the Foreign Office presumed this qualification did not apply to the Sunni Moslem financial adviser Ibn Saud had requested from the British to help organize Saudi finances, on the grounds that the Saudi Treasury was located in Mecca and that no non-Moslem could live or work there. Finally, with regard to the economic or financial mission that the State Department had referred to in its proposal, the Foreign Office declared that to its knowledge Saudi Arabia had not requested one. If the issue arose, then London believed the leadership of the mission should be determined by whichever nation had the preponderant interest in the Saudi economy at the time.

This seeming straightforward response was in effect a complete rejection of the compromise American plan. Whereas the United States interpreted its position with regard to the Saudi oil concession as giving it the predominant interest in the Saudi economy, London could and did argue that the then-current level of oil production was relatively small compared to other Saudi trade and financial activities, and that Britain hence should have the greater say. This was not a position the Roosevelt administration was prepared to accept, and back to London went a firm American rejoinder. The State Department on July 1, 1944, informed the Foreign Office that, recognizing the Near East as an area of primary British military responsibility, the United States had given its approval to a British officer heading the military mission. This was contingent, however, on an American heading any financial or economic mission and the stipulation applied to any financial or economic adviser or mission, regardless of how the British or Saudis choose to describe it. Moreover, while Ibn Saud obviously had the last word in determining the nature of the advisers sent him, the supplying nations also had the duty to clearly make their wishes known. Finally, should the location of the Saudi Treasury in Mecca prove to be the obstacle to appointment of a non-Moslem adviser, the State Department pointed out that the Saudi Treasury could always be moved, or the adviser work with Saudi officials sent to deal with him in Jidda.[6]

Not unexpectedly the British found the new American role as distasteful as the earlier one. On July 21, 1944, the reply came back, transmitted by the American embassy in London. The Foreign Office concentrated its fire on the argument that the preponderant interest in the Saudi Arabian economy was unquestionably American in character. The British attempted to refute this, pointing out that most of the export activities of Saudi merchants were directed toward British territories and sterling area countries. Moreover, Britain (because of its administration of India) was the largest Moslem power and a large proportion of the pilgrims to Mecca and Medina, whose expenditures provided a major share of Saudi revenues, came from British possessions. As against this, the Foreign Office contended, the American contribution to the economic life of Saudi Arabia was very limited, even including the royalties from Aramco. Accordingly, the British viewed the American claim to preponderance in the Saudi Arabian economy as based upon a misconception. Although the situation would undoubtedly change as Saudi oil production increased, the Foreign Office suggested that the respective roles of the United States and Britain in Saudi Arabia could be reappraised at that time.

In the midst of this controversy, both London and Washington were suddenly faced with the fact that the Saudi economic situation was rapidly worsening, and that a serious threat to the stability of the country might follow if they could not quickly agree on a coordinated program of aid. On June 17, 1944, King Ibn Saud asked the American and British legations in Jidda to transmit word to their respective governments that economic assistance was vitally needed and that if it were not provided rapidly disorders might result. Asked for additional details by the legations, the acting Saudi foreign minister reported five days later that deaths by starvation were occurring in the southern Hejaz and that his government had suspended food sales because of depleted stocks. By July 7, 1944, the situation had so deteriorated that the acting foreign minister told the American legation that government stocks of wheat and flour would be exhausted in about three days.

Faced with this crisis, the controversy between Washington and London for primacy in Saudi Arabia was put aside. On June 26, 1944, the State Department had become so concerned over the activities of the British minister in Jidda that Secretary of State Hull summoned the British ambassador in Washington to advise him that the United States could not put up with efforts to injure the American government's relations with Ibn Saud. By July 12, 1944, however, the emphasis had changed to one of cooperation with the British to alleviate the distress in Saudi Arabia. On that day, the American minister in Jidda was informed that both Washington and London were instructing their representatives in Saudi Arabia that a joint Anglo-American program for financial and material aid had been agreed upon, and that this would be regarded as the expression of a single combined policy on the part of the two governments. The minister was further instructed to treat all requests for aid from Saudi Arabia jointly with his British colleague and to cooperate with him wholeheartedly.[7]

At the same time the policy dispute was being papered over, both Washington and London agreed on the help to be furnished the Saudis. On August 1, 1944, the American and British representatives advised the king that emergency aid would be provided, to include 40,000 tons of cereals, 4,500 tons of dates, and 3,000 tons of sugar. Additionally, the United States and Britain agreed to maintain a three months' supply of cereals, tea, and sugar in Saudi Arabia at all times, with the United States to provide silver for Saudi coinage and Britain funds for the operation of Saudi diplomatic missions abroad.

Once the joint aid program was established, the difference between British and Americans regarding Saudi Arabia, probably abetted by its efforts to deal with each of the great powers separately, resurfaced. On August 6, 1944, the American minister in Jidda reported the king's reaction to the aid package. Although Ibn Saud expressed his gratitude, he stressed his conviction that it was insufficient, that the Saudi government was in a grave financial plight, and that it was unable to pay its obligations, with official salaries several months in arrears.

Washington was disposed to accept the king's arguments, advising London on August 14, 1944, that it felt this must be done in the absence of accurate statistical data to the contrary. The British, however, were very reluctant to increase the amount of help, asserting that the Saudis were requesting excess quantities. On August 16, 1944, the British minister in Jidda protested to his American colleague that Washington had broken the promise to cooperate on aid to the Saudis by unilaterally increasing its assistance.

In September 1944 Washington named Colonel William Eddy as minister in Jidda, to replace Moose, but no improvement followed in the relations between the British and American legations. Shortly after his arrival Eddy met with the British minister, Stanley R. Jordan, and was informed straightaway that a highly qualified Indian Moslem had already been selected and was available to serve as financial adviser to Ibn Saud whenever the Western governments agreed, that the British military mission was being expanded, and that a British bank had requested Saudi permission to open a branch in that country. Eddy was understandably distressed and concluded that the latter development was clearly aimed at countering a recent move by the National City Bank of New York to do so.

Eddy next met with the king's private secretary, who was also serving as deputy foreign minister. Not unexpectedly, the latter stressed to the American minister the necessity for establishing intimate Saudi-American relations. Declaring that he wished to speak to Eddy on a subject of the greatest importance and in the strictest confidence, he stressed that Ibn Saud was convinced of the personal friendship of President Roosevelt. However, America's declaration that it was willing to grant aid to Saudi Arabia had been followed by a reduction in British assistance, so that the total was less than the amount identified before the United States offer. If the State Department was prepared to let its aid to Saudi Arabia be reduced and shaped by London's wishes, then Saudi Arabia would have to yield to British influence and desires, not merely to please an ally but to survive. Moreover, the king was concerned that the United States might lose interest in his country and retire to domestic preoccupations, as happened after previous wars. Even more to be feared was the possibility that Washington's policy might fall under control of the Zionists. Although it did not wish to cease cooperating with Great Britain, Saudi Arabia hoped that there might be a large area where it and the United States could collaborate alone, going beyond the end of the war. The Saudis refused to give any specific details as to what the suggested cooperation would entail, and Eddy could agree only to convey the message to the State Department for its consideration. In retrospect, it appears likely that this plea for a special relationship was meant by the king to encompass an American military and economic guarantee for the independence and development of Saudi Arabia, with the United States furnishing protection and financial aid in return for Saudi oil. This was a suggestion that Ibn Saud was to make several times in the future, in less veiled form.

Meanwhile, relations between the American and British legations in Jidda continued to deteriorate. On November 24, 1944, Eddy asked the State Department to remove the injunction upon him to meet with Saudi officials on aid matters only in the company of the British, reporting that the British minister constantly discussed United States affairs privately with the Saudi government and that the United States legation should be free to follow suit.

Four days later he warned Washington that he was convinced the British minister would take the lead in an effort to embroil the United States in difficulties with the king by proposing a drastic reduction in the joint subsidy. To counter this, Eddy recommended that if the British insisted on an unreasonable reduction in the subsidy, the United States cease participating in it and instead assist the Saudi government independently.[8]

In the face of these developments, the State Department moved to protect American interests. On December 9, 1944, Eddy was instructed to defer discussions with the British until he could meet personally with the king and to refuse to concur in any British proposals on a joint assistance package that he felt was inadequate to meet Saudi needs. This was made even more explicit in guidance sent the minister on December 24, 1944, in which he was told explicitly not to inform the British minister before seeing the king. Instead, shortly before Eddy's scheduled private meeting with Ibn Saud, the State Department proposed to inform the British embassy in Washington of the general nature of the subjects he would discuss with the king and of the fact that the British minister in Jidda was not being informed because of his apparent deliberate failure to cooperate with Eddy in similar matters.

The new hard line with regard to the British in Saudi Arabia in fact reflected a high-level policy decision in Washington. After consulting with Secretary of War Stimson and Secretary of the Navy Forrestal and obtaining their agreement on the importance of Saudi Arabia to the United States, both during and after the war, Secretary of State Hull wrote a memorandum to President Roosevelt stressing this point and requesting the president's approval for a program of long-range American aid to that country. Sent to the president on December 22, 1944, the memorandum noted that Saudi Arabia was dependent for survival upon help from abroad and that if the United States did not supply it, undoubtedly some other nation would. This in turn might permit that nation (that is, Britain) to acquire a dominant position in Saudi Arabia inimical to the welfare of Saudi Arabia and to the national interest of the United States. Pointing out that Ibn Saud had indicated his preference for American aid in preference to assistance from other countries, Hull urged Roosevelt to approve a program of support to Saudi Arabia. Not only would Congress be asked to appropriate funds for the purpose, apart from Lend-Lease, but the president of the Export-Import Bank would be requested to agree to provide long-term developmental loans to Saudi Arabia, and the American Army and Navy directed to give immediate consideration to requests from Jidda for assistance.[9]

The secretary of state met with President Roosevelt to discuss the matter on December 23, 1944, and obtained from him tentative approval to proceed.[10] The projected total of American aid to Saudi Arabia discussed was from $28 million to $57 million in the five-year period from 1945 to 1950, with congressional approval to be obtained because the Lend-Lease program was set to end as of July 1945. The American minister to Jidda conveyed word of the planned new American aid program to King Ibn Saud in a private audience on January 1, 1945, and reported the king's pleasure. Although World War II, the occasion for the great expansion in American interest in Saudi Arabia, was now approaching its end, Washington's ties with that nation were slated to continue and even to expand. A new period of American relations with Saudi Arabia was about to begin.

ENDNOTES

1. *Foreign Relations, 1944,* Washington, D.C., 1965, Vol. V, p. 675.

2. *Ibid.,* pp. 679-684.

3. *Ibid.,* pp. 685-691.

4. *Ibid.,* p. 694.

5. *Ibid.,* pp. 696-702.

6. *Ibid.,* pp. 704-713.

7. *Ibid.,* pp. 716-719.

8. *Ibid.,* pp. 734-753.

9. *Ibid.,* pp. 754-758.

10. *Foreign Relations, 1945,* Washington, D.C., 1969, Vol. VIII, p. 847.

CHAPTER 6
Amid Problems, the American Presence Grows

Benson Lee Grayson

As World War II approached its end, the expansion of American influence in Saudi Arabia was not without significant obstructions. The two major roadblocks were the continued rivalry between the United States and Great Britain for primacy in the area and the growing Saudi suspicion about Washington's support for a Jewish homeland in Palestine. The latter element was emphasized in the briefings given President Roosevelt by the State Department in December 1944 as he prepared for a personal meeting with King Ibn Saud.

Coincidental with his approval of the program of long-range assistance to Saudi Arabia, the president was engaged in preparations for a Big Three conference with the British Prime Minister, Winston Churchill, and Soviet Prime Minister Joseph Stalin to be held at Yalta in February 1945. Taking advantage of the president's presence in the region, the State Department proposed that Roosevelt meet with the king of Egypt, the emperor of Ethiopia, and King Ibn Saud on his way back from the Soviet Union.

In his briefings, the president was cautioned about the continued disagreement between the Arabs and Jews over the status of Palestine and about the difficulty in trying to find a position on the dispute that would not anger one or both parties. On January 9, 1945, Undersecretary of State Stettinius showed him a report from Eddy in Jidda describing Ibn Saud's state of mind. In the report, Eddy quoted the king as urging the formation of an Arab military alliance to protect the member states against aggression and calling for a joint commitment by the Arab states to defend Palestine against Zionism by force if necessary. Ibn Saud further declared that he would be honored to die on the battlefield as a champion of the Palestine Arabs. Eddy urged that with Axis radio propaganda grossly exaggerating American official support of Zionism, any pro-Zionist move by Washington would be most unfortunate.

No more comforting was a memorandum sent to the president on January 17, 1945, by James M. Landis, Director of American Economic Operations in the Middle East. Landis, who had worked with the British in Cairo in framing the program of joint economic assistance to Saudi Arabia, informed the president that he had given much thought to what Roosevelt might say to Ibn Saud about a solution to the Palestine problem. Landis began by noting that the king felt very strongly about the matter, had refused, to date, all suggestions from the United States that there might be some middle ground, and recently in the presence of a member of Landis's staff had threatened to see to the execution of any Jew who might seek to enter his country. The director added that Ibn Saud politically represented the Wahhabis sect, which was the spearhead of the pan Islam movement and was unwilling to have any dealings with infidels, let alone Jews, and that Ibn Saud had had to defend himself against charges of being friendly to Christians and of admitting them to Saudi Arabia. For these reasons, Landis concluded that any suggestion by the president concerning Palestine that did not go to the root of the problem had no chance of success. He recommended the president give up any idea that Palestine could become a Jewish state as distinct from a Jewish homeland, and that Jewish immigration into Palestine be related to the economic absorptive capacity of Palestine rather than to the political issue of a Jewish minority or majority.[1]

The warning conveyed by Landis to the president was reinforced on January 31, 1945, by comments made by Ibn Saud to officers of the American legation. Warning that the United States and Britain had a free choice for Palestine between an Arab land of peace or a Jewish land drenched in blood, he declared that the Jews then there could stay, but that no more could be admitted. If America chose in favor of the Jews, whom the king characterized as "accursed in the Koran as enemies of the Moslems until the end of the world," it would indicate that America had repudiated its friendship for Saudi Arabia.

From the Zionist side, the Roosevelt administration was also subjected to strong pressures. On February 1, 1945, Dr. Stephen S. Wise, Chairman of the American Zionist Emergency Council, called upon Acting Secretary of State Joseph C. Grew. Dr. Wise stressed the need to ensure large-scale Jewish immigration into Palestine from Romania and elsewhere in Europe, where the Jewish communities were threatened with extinction at the hands of the Germans. The Zionist leader warned that only some 1,500 Jews a month were permitted to enter Palestine, and that even that small flow was scheduled to be cut off by the British within four months. He added that he had already raised the problem with President Roosevelt, and that the latter was taking a memorandum prepared by Dr. Wise to his forthcoming meeting with Winston Churchill, whom the Zionist leader characterized as being thoroughly sympathetic on the Palestine problem.[2]

At the Yalta Big Three Conference, which lasted from February 3 to February 11, 1945, the bulk of the discussions concerned bringing the war in Europe to a successful conclusion, the postwar administration of the former Axis powers, and Soviet entry into the war against Japan. Palestine was mentioned only in passing. At a dinner for the Big Three leaders on February 10, 1945, President Roosevelt declared that he was a Zionist, to which Marshall

Stalin replied that he was one in principle but that he recognized the difficulty of a Jewish state. On the following day after the departure of the Big Three leaders, the foreign ministers met to approve final papers summarizing the findings of the conference. At this meeting British Foreign Secretary Anthony Eden, supported by Secretary of State Stettinius, who had replaced Cordell Hull as Secretary on December 1, 1944, urged that Saudi Arabia be included among those countries that, if they declared war on the Axis before March 1, 1945, would be invited to attend the founding conference of the United Nations at San Francisco.[3] Although the Soviet foreign minister refused to agree to this proposal before discussing it with Stalin, President Roosevelt did pass on the suggestion to King Ibn Saud. The king acted upon it, declaring war against the Axis as of March 1, 1945, and subsequently sent a delegation to the United Nations conference. This marked a clear departure from the previous Saudi isolationist stance. Interestingly, even as late as the Yalta conference, it was Britain and not the United States that took the lead in recommending Saudi membership in the United Nations.

Upon conclusion of the Yalta conference, President Roosevelt flew to Cairo, where he boarded the American Navy cruiser *Quincy*. His meeting with King Ibn Saud took place on board the vessel, near the Suez Canal. The king, who at the age of 65 was leaving his country for the first time, was transported to the site from Jidda by the American destroyer *Murphy*, sleeping in a tent on deck and taking with him live sheep to be slaughtered for food.

Despite the exotic aspects of the meeting between the king and the president on February 14, 1945, it went off well. Roosevelt in fact raised the delicate topic of the Jews, but in a diplomatic fashion, asking Ibn Saud for his advice regarding the Jewish refugees who had been driven from their homes in Europe. The king suggested that they return to their countries of origin or, if this were impossible, that they be given living space in the Axis countries that had oppressed them. Ibn Saud then turned to Palestine, stating that the Arabs there would defend their legitimate rights against any influx of Jews and would die rather than yield their lands. So far as the king was concerned, the most worthwhile outcome of the meeting was a pledge by the president that he would do nothing to assist the Jews against the Arabs and would make no move hostile to the Arab people. Roosevelt also gave assurances with regard to Syria and Lebanon, which the Arabs feared France might continue to occupy, although the latter had pledged their independence. Roosevelt promised that if the French government reneged, the United States would give Syria and Lebanon all possible support short of force.[4]

In contrast to his meeting with the president, Ibn Saud's discussions with Winston Churchill went poorly. Learning that Roosevelt was to meet with the Arabian king only a few days before the scheduled date, the British leader tried unsuccessfully to see Ibn Saud first, ultimately having to settle for a meeting three days later. According to the account Ibn Saud gave privately to the American minister in Jidda, Churchill attempted to pressure the king, noting that Britain had supported and subsidized Ibn Saud for twenty years and had made possible the stability of his reign by fending off potential enemies on his frontiers. Because Britain had seen him through his difficult days, Britain was now entitled to request Saudi assistance in the problem of Palestine. The king could help restrain fanatical Arab elements, insist on moderation in the Arab councils, and bring about a realistic compromise with Zionism. Both sides would have to make concessions and Britain looked to Ibn Saud to help prepare the Arab concessions.

> Ibn Saud stressed to the minister his unhappiness over Churchill's proposal. The king stated that he had flatly refused, telling Churchill that he would always be a friend to Britain. However, what the Prime Minister was asking would be an act of treachery to the Prophet and to all believing Moslems which would wipe out his honor and destroy his soul. Specifically, the king refused to acquiesce in a compromise with Zionism much less take any initiative. Instead, Ibn Saud asked the British leader to promise that Jewish immigration to Palestine would be stopped. In turn, Churchill refused, despite the king's warning that a struggle to death between Arabs and Jews would occur if unreasonable Jewish immigration to Palestine were renewed.[5]

After his return to Washington, the president continued to indicate his favorable opinion of Ibn Saud. At an informal lunch on March 5, 1945, with Mrs. Roosevelt and with Colonel Hoskins, then serving as economic adviser to the legation in Egypt, Saudi Arabia, and other nearby countries, the president characterized Winston Churchill as being as strongly pro-Zionist as ever. When Mrs. Roosevelt commented on the fact that the Zionists felt much stronger and might risk a fight with the Arabs over Palestine, the president reminded her that there were more than 15,000,000 Arabs in and around Palestine and that, in the long run, those numbers would win out. Subsequently, in a conversation with a State Department official on March 15, 1945, the president described his meeting with Ibn Saud. Roosevelt commented that he told the king that Saudi Arabia was a good example of a country that needed to increase its purchasing power, adding that he (Roosevelt) was essentially a businessman, that he had been the head of a big insurance company, the Maryland Casualty, and that as a businessman he had always been very much interested in Saudi Arabia. Roosevelt had gone on to say that he knew a considerable amount of the history of Arabia, that Arabia needed irrigation projects, and that if he were in the pump business, he would regard Arabia as a great potential market. He stated that the development of irrigation projects would increase the productivity of the land and considerably increase the purchasing power of the country.

The president's liking for Ibn Saud and his knowledge of Saudi Arabia notwithstanding, he was fully aware of the strong support within the United States for the idea of a Jewish homeland in Palestine. On March 16, 1945, he met again with Dr. Stephen Wise, the Zionist leader, and authorized the latter to say that the president had made clear his position concerning Zionism in a letter written in October 1944. The letter in question, to Democratic Senator Robert F. Wagner of New York State, gave the president's full endorsement to the 1944 Democratic Party platform plank that supported unrestricted Jewish immigration to Palestine and the establishment there of a free and democratic Jewish state.

Picked up by the American and foreign press, the president's statement of support for a Jewish state in Palestine caused widespread anger and demonstrations in the Arab world. Aware of the probable adverse Arab reaction, the director of the Office of Near Eastern and African Affairs checked with the White House and learned that the president had indeed authorized Dr. Wise's statement. In a memorandum to the acting secretary of state on March 20, 1945, the director warned that the president's statement would have serious repercussions in the Near East and specifically undo most of the good effect of the president's meeting with Ibn Saud. Moreover, the president's continued support of Zionism, the memorandum continued, could lead to actual bloodshed in the Near East between Arabs and Jews and endanger the security of the immensely valuable oil concession in Saudi Arabia. It could even throw the Arabs into the arms of the Soviets, who had indicated they opposed a Jewish state in Palestine.[6]

In response to anti-American demonstrations in the Near East and the recommendations from the State Department, the president moved to further clarify his position on Palestine. In a letter to Ibn Saud on April 5, 1945, Roosevelt declared that he remained committed to the promise that he had given the king at their February meeting, that the United States would take no move hostile to the Arabs and that Washington's position was that no decision be taken with respect to the basic situation in Palestine without full consultation with both Arabs and Jews. If there appeared to be some contradiction between the two presidential statements, Washington hoped that it could nonetheless avoid the unwelcome prospect of angering either the Arabs or the Jews.

A week after signing his letter to King Ibn Saud, on April 12, 1945, President Roosevelt died and was succeeded in the White House by his vice president, Harry Truman. The latter was more inclined than President Roosevelt to be sympathetic to the Zionist hopes for a Jewish state in Palestine and tended to ignore contrary recommendations from the State Department along the lines given his predecessor. On April 18, 1945, Secretary of State Stettinius wrote to the new president, warning him that Zionist leaders would try to obtain from him at an early date commitments in favor of the Zionist aims of unlimited Jewish immigration into Palestine and the establishment there of a Jewish state. The secretary noted that while the United States had every sympathy for the persecuted Jews of Europe, the question of Palestine was a highly complex one, involving questions that went far beyond the plight of the Jews of Europe. He stressed that the tense state of the Near East required that the Palestine question be handled with the greatest care and with a view to the long-range interests of the United States. Acting Secretary of State Joseph Grew followed this up with an even more specific warning on May 1, 1945, advising the president that although Roosevelt at times expressed views sympathetic to Zionist aims, he had also given assurances to the Arabs, which they regarded as definite commitments by the United States. Grew further called Truman's attention to the assurances given by President Roosevelt to Ibn Saud at their personal meeting in February 1945 and in his letter to the king of April 5, 1945, attaching copies. In closing, Grew declared that the Arabs of the whole Near East had made no secret of their hostility to Zionism, and that President Roosevelt understood this clearly, having remarked that a Jewish state in Palestine could be established and maintained only by military force.[7]

Notwithstanding the cautious advice from the State Department, by the summer of 1945 President Truman made public statements on Palestine that aroused Saudi Arabia and the other Arab states. After returning from the Big Three meeting held at Potsdam, East Germany, from July 17 to August 2, 1945, President Truman told a press conference on August 16, 1945, that he favored admitting as many Jews as possible into Palestine, although he had no desire to send 500,000 American troops to maintain the peace there and felt the matter had to be worked out by the British and the Arabs. On September 26, 1945, the president further angered the Arabs when, in response to a question at a press conference, he stated that he had found no record of any commitment given by President Roosevelt to Saudi Arabia not to support Jewish claims on Palestine. Finally, in a letter to British Prime Minister Clement Attlee, whose Labor government was elected to power in Britain in July 1945, Truman urged on August 31, 1945, that an additional 100,000 Jewish survivors of the Nazi extermination program in Europe be permitted to enter Palestine and then publicly referred to this request on October 18, 1945.

The Arab reaction to the president's statements was predictable and adverse. In Jidda the Saudi foreign minister informed Colonel Eddy that in case a search of State Department records failed to reveal any pledge by President Roosevelt to King Ibn Saud concerning Palestine, the ruler was prepared to publish the letter dated April 5, 1945, that he had received from the president containing it. The State Department was most apprehensive over the effect the president's statements might have upon American relations with the Arab nations. On October 2, 1945, Acting Secretary of State Dean Acheson forwarded a memorandum to the president warning that his proposal to admit 100,000 Jewish refugees into Palestine would, if adopted, constitute a basic change in the Palestine situation, which President Roosevelt had pledged would not take place without consultation with the Arabs and Jews. The memorandum adds that the failure of the United States to carry out its promises would constitute the severest kind of blow to American prestige in the Near East and elsewhere and seriously threaten American vital interests in the Arab world.[8]

In response to the outcry he had stimulated, President Truman modified his position. In a letter to King Ibn Saud on October 13, 1945, he advised the monarch that he would publicly state President Roosevelt had given assurances to the king and make available to the press the text of Roosevelt's letter of April 5, 1945. In a related move, Truman told a press conference on October 18, 1945, that the matter of the homeless Jews in Europe was still under consideration, and should any proposals emerge that would change the basic situation in Palestine, the United States would not reach a final conclusion on them without full consultation with both the Arabs and Jews.

The new American stance did not fully dispel the suspicion of the United States in Saudi Arabia. On October 26, 1945, Eddy, temporarily in the United States, warned the State Department that if Jidda's growing concern that Washington was flirting with a Palestine policy friendly to Zionism should be confirmed, American enterprises in Saudi Arabia would be seriously handicapped. In the following month Ibn Saud pointedly referred at a public gathering to Britain as the Arabs' best friend, reflecting the less sympathetic attitude toward Jewish immigration into Palestine that the Attlee government had espoused.

In the face of Saudi apprehension over the Truman administration's attitude on Palestine, it might have been expected that Saudi-American relations would suffer. Some erosion in confidence did occur, but the expansion of a wide range of ties between the two countries was only temporarily arrested. The simple fact was that Ibn Saud recognized that his nation needed the backing of a friendly great power. Whereas before the war Great Britain had filled that role, by 1945 it had become apparent that London's capability and willingness to maintain its prewar position in the Middle East no longer existed. In the absence of a British alternative, the Saudis had no choice but to look to Washington for support.

As noted previously, the United States government had concluded in December 1944 that America's vital interests would be served by entering into a long-term program of assistance to Saudi Arabia. In February 1945, subsequent to President Roosevelt's meeting with Ibn Saud, representatives of the State, War, and Navy departments agreed upon a comprehensive plan of aid to the Saudis, aimed at ensuring continued American access to the Saudi oil fields. To achieve this end, the War Department would immediately offer to construct military airfields and improve roads in Saudi Arabia and to dispatch a military mission larger in scope than that under Colonel Shomber, which had arrived in 1944 and whose training had largely been confined to ground force operations. Similarly, the United States Export-Import Bank would consider financing long-term developmental projects in Saudi Arabia.

Initially, the American plans were based on the assumption that Great Britain would participate equally in providing a joint aid package to Saudi Arabia, as it had done the previous year. On April 17, 1945, however, the British embassy in Washington delivered a memorandum to the State Department stating that the British government had decided that its subsidy for 1945 could not exceed $5 million. Hence, because London did not want either the United States or Britain to provide more than 50 percent of the joint subsidy, the total package could not exceed $10 million. The memorandum concluded that of course the United States could provide a greater sum if it desired, but that Britain strongly recommended against it on the grounds that abandonment of the principle of equal partnership would inevitably give the impression of an Anglo-American rivalry, which both governments were so eager to avoid.

If the Foreign Office thought that it could persuade the United States to go along with a smaller joint subsidy, it was seriously mistaken. Notified of the British memorandum by the State Department, Colonel Eddy cabled from Jidda on April 20, 1945, that he was relieved to learn that the British government would not stand in the way of the United States economic assistance to Saudi Arabia in 1945. He described Ibn Saud as being troubled and indignant at having heard nothing definite concerning the 1945 subsidy or material assistance program and warned that the king would regard any joint communication proposing a subsidy at the level suggested by the British as confirming his fears that the United States could not be relied upon.

The State Department, too, concluded that despite London's position, a higher level of American aid was warranted. On April 24, 1945, the State Department answered the British embassy memorandum, stating that it could not accept the proposal of a $10-million joint subsidy because it considered $16 million to be the minimum sum needed to meet vital Saudi requirements, which would still be less than the $20 million in assistance furnished in 1944. Accordingly, although the United States valued the concept of a joint program and wanted to continue British participation, if London unhappily concluded that it could not go beyond $5 million in aid, then the United States was prepared to provide unilaterally what it considered to be the amount of assistance necessary.[9]

Coincidentally, at the same time the United States was in essence rejecting the British position on the joint subsidy, it was asking London to approve American plans to build an airfield at Dhahran. The airfield in question was regarded in Washington as desirable, not only to facilitate military flights to the Far East to assist in pursuit of the war against Japan, but also as a token of American interest in aiding Saudi Arabia. Perhaps surprisingly, in view of Washington's attitude on the subsidy matter, London gave its approval to American construction of the Dhahran base in April 1945. With London's agreement obtained, the American minister in Jidda raised the matter of the Dhahran airfield with the king in the context of the larger package of American aid. On May 13, 1945, he was able to inform the State Department that

Ibn Saud had granted permission for construction of the airfield, provided that it would be transferred to Saudi control immediately after the end of the war. The United States would have use of the field for an additional three years, with American commercial aircraft to be granted use on a most-favored-nation basis when the field was opened to commercial traffic.

At this point, with Saudi and British approval obtained, the State Department decided that it might be better to have President Truman's approval for the concept of a long-term American aid program for Saudi Arabia before proceeding further. In view of the department's concerns that the new president might intend a shift in America policy vis-a-vis Palestine and the Arabs, this was a sound precaution. Therefore, on May 23, 1945, Acting Secretary of State Joseph Grew sent President Truman a memorandum summarizing the aid package for Saudi Arabia that President Roosevelt had agreed to in December 1944. After a briefing from Assistant Secretary of State Dean Acheson and the undersecretary of the Navy, stressing the importance of Saudi oil to the United States, President Truman on May 29, 1945, tentatively approved the aid plan.[10]

The approval of Saudi Arabia, Great Britain, President Truman, and the State Department notwithstanding, the American aid program faced further delays. The first administrative snag surfaced on June 14, 1945, when the British counselor in Washington privately informed the State Department that he was in difficulty with his own government because of his recommendation that the British approve American construction of the airfield at Dhahran. Although the original discussions had centered on an American military airfield at Dhahran, the British government was now disturbed to learn that Washington had changed signals and had obtained Saudi permission to use the facility for commercial aircraft also. London feared this would lead to unwelcome competition for its commercial companies serving the area. Embarrassed, the State Department apologized and explained that although there had been a change in American policy, it had construed Britain's approval as covering commercial use of the airfield as well. In any event, the State Department believed that commercial facilities obtained by American airlines would not hurt the British, because the installation would be open to all foreign airlines on a nondiscriminatory basis. Moreover, the State Department pointed out, in view of what it considered to be the obstructive British tactics throughout the Middle East to prevent American airlines from operating, the United States was not prepared to accept the likely delay in having Eddy withhold his discussions with the king on the subject until he could receive the concurrence from the British legation in Jidda.[11]

The State Department now encountered more serious problems in the shape of administrative difficulties in Washington. Congressional hearings on the foreign aid program did not start until mid-June, and on June 18, 1945, the State Department informed the American legation in Jidda that final congressional approval might not be obtained before

June 30, or even later. For this reason, it urged Eddy to advise the king that it might be a matter of months before the administration would know the exact level of American assistance that could be provided over the next several years. The department added that a long-range financial assistance program of the type desired by the king was without precedent in American history, and the fact that it was being considered was in itself proof of the great interest the United States had in the king's problems and the welfare of his people.

As if this problem were not enough, the American view of the airfield to be built at Dhahran had now changed. Although Washington had previously pressed the British and Saudis to agree to construction of the field, a change in plans for deploying troops from Europe to the Pacific diminished the need for the base. On June 25, 1945, the State Department cabled Eddy that the War Department now considered the expenditure of funds for a field at Dhahran on the basis of military necessity to be of doubtful legal validity. Plans could of course proceed on the basis of the importance of the project to American national interest, but no action could be taken on the project until the president gave his approval to the new justification.

Receiving these unwelcome tidings, Eddy at once informed the State Department that the Saudis could not help concluding that the United States was an undependable ally. On June 21, 1945, he warned that Ibn Saud would probably react to news of the aid delay by bleeding Aramco for loans to stabilize his nation's economy. For its part the department of State was not unaware of the danger. In an effort to circumvent the congressional delay, the department obtained Export-Import Bank approval to consider development loans to Saudi Arabia apart from the question of the long-range budgetary assistance program. At the same time, President Truman was briefed on the political ramifications of failing to construct the Dhahran airfield and gave his approval for work on the project to begin, notwithstanding the lessened military justification for it.

Happily, much of the concern over an expected adverse Saudi reaction to the delay in implementing an American aid program turned out to have been unjustified. On July 4, 1945, Eddy informed Washington that Ibn Saud had unexpectedly declined the offer of an American military mission, preferring to have foreign assistance in developing his country obtained via civilian agencies. The minister added that the king's decision was based on his desire to avoid criticism by fanatical reactionaries in his country who would have attacked any foreign presence, abuse from his Hashemite neighbors who would have proclaimed him a puppet maintained in power by foreigners, and objections from the British to a military mission in which they were not at least equal partners.[12]

Despite the king's rejection of the American military mission plan, events were clearly working in favor of the expansion of United States influence in Saudi Arabia. The primary factor was the changed position and policy of Washington's main rival for preeminence in the area—Great Britain. The war had wreaked havoc with Britain's economic strength. By the fall of 1945, London was desperately seeking financial assistance from the United States, successfully obtaining a $4.4-billion loan in December 1945. As a supplicant for American aid, the British were less disposed to challenge Washington's policies concerning Saudi Arabia, particularly since that country was accorded a lower priority by the Foreign Office than others in the Middle East in which the British presence had been traditionally stronger. Although at the Potsdam Big Three meeting on July 22, 1945, British Prime Minister Winston Churchill had declared that his nation would have the responsibility for keeping the peace in Saudi Arabia, this was no more than a reflex gesture of a policy already dead. Earlier in the month his government had been forced to inform the State Department that financial stringency prevented it from giving more than $5 million in aid to Saudi Arabia in 1945, accepting the fact that Washington would provide a greater sum and garner the greater influence. Moreover, the incoming Labor government of Clement Attlee, which defeated Churchill in the general election in July 1945, was less ready than its predecessor to devote scarce resources to maintaining intact Britain's far-flung empire and was more willing to surrender to America responsibility for defending Western interests in Saudi Arabia.

The Truman administration, for its part, was quite prepared to take over the British responsibilities there. On July 29, 1945, Eddy, together with the British minister, called upon the Saudi minister of finance and acting foreign minister, Sheikh Abdullah Suleiman. After the two envoys explained their respective governments' agreement to participate equally in the joint $410-million aid program, the British minister expressed London's regret that it could not provide additional support. Then, with obvious satisfaction at having won his struggle, Eddy formally notified the Saudi government that Washington would separately grant an additional $6 million in assistance in currency and commodities.[13]

Ibn Saud was no less eager to see an expansion of United States influence in his country. On July 31, 1945, his son, Foreign Minister Faisal, again visited Washington, taking the opportunity presented by his attendance at the United Nations conference in San Francisco. Because the president and secretary of state were out of Washington, Faisal was received by Acting Secretary Joseph Grew. The foreign minister was eager to stress the friendship and confidence the king felt toward the United States and declared that Saudi Arabia was permitting American citizens to engage in activities that had not been allowed the nationals of any other great power. Faisal cautioned that his father could not move too rapidly without strengthening the hand of his traditionalist enemies and that it was for this reason that he had terminated the American military training mission. He also underscored the great importance the Saudis attached to developments in Palestine and urged that the United States not support any policy that would deprive the Arabs in Palestine of their rights or place them under the dominance of a Jewish government.

The success of the foreign minister's talks in Washington and the expanded American aid package were almost immediately reflected in a more responsive attitude on the part of the Saudis. On August 6, 1945, the royal government immediately accepted the American proposal to construct the proposed airbase at Dhahran. Given the closed nature of its society, the terms accepted by Saudi Arabia were extremely generous. In an unprecedented break with past Saudi practices, it granted the United States the right to build, use, operate, and maintain a base, not to exceed an area of twenty-five square miles, and to put there two runways and facilities for a complement of 500 persons. Although the base was described in the agreement as intended for use in the war against Japan, Washington was given the right to use it for a period of three years after the end of hostilities. Moreover, some 3,500 foreigners, including 500 Americans, could be brought into the country to build the base.

The end of the war with Japan on August 14, 1945, brought no reduction in the growing American-Saudi ties. Despite the cessation of hostilities, the secretaries of State, War, and Navy recommended that construction of the Dhahran base be completed. President Truman approved this finding on September 28, 1945. He also specifically exempted Saudi Arabia from inclusion in the general worldwide termination of American Lend-Lease aid, which followed close upon the end of the war.

The new, long-term American interest in Saudi Arabia was also evident in the planning undertaken by the State Department to provide continued financial support to that country. Following the president's decision in May 1945 to embark on the program, the department drew up a plan under which the United States would supply up to $25 million in financial assistance over a five-year period ending in December 1950.[14] In its way, this was as much of a break with previous American foreign policy as the Saudi agreement to the Dhahran airbase had been for that country. Never before in its history had the United States undertaken to provide such economic assistance to a foreign state in peacetime. More was to follow. The growth of American-Saudi relations in the postwar world had only begun.

ENDNOTES

1. *Foreign Relations, 1945,* Washington, D.C., 1969, Vol. VIII, pp. 679-682.

2. *Ibid.,* pp. 687-689.

3. *Foreign Relations, Conferences at Malta and Yalta,* Washington, D.C., 1955, p. 931.

4. *Foreign Relations, 1945,* Washington, D.C., 1969, Vol. VIII, pp. 2-4.

5. *Ibid.,* pp. 689-690.

6. *Ibid.,* pp. 690-695.

7. *Ibid.,* pp. 698-706.

8. *Ibid.,* pp. 737-755.

9. *Ibid.,* pp. 875-884.

10. *Ibid.,* pp. 902-903.

11. *Ibid.,* pp. 905-915.

12. *Ibid.,* pp. 915-920.

13. *Ibid.,* pp. 935-936.

14. *Ibid.,* pp. 960-963.

CHAPTER 7
The Defense of Saudi Arabia[1]

George H. W. Bush

In the life of a nation, we're called upon to define who we are and what we believe. Sometimes these choices are not easy. But today as president, I ask for your support in a decision I've made to stand up for what's right and condemn what's wrong—all in the cause of peace.

At my direction, elements of the 82nd Airborne Division, as well as key units of the United States Air Force, are arriving today to take up defensive positions in Saudi Arabia. I took this action to assist the Saudi Arabian government in the defense of its homeland.

No one commits America's Armed Forces to a dangerous mission lightly. But after perhaps unparalleled international consultation and exhausting every alternative, it became necessary to take this action. Let me tell you why.

Less than a week ago, in the early morning hours of August 2nd, Iraqi armed forces, without provocation or warning, invaded a peaceful Kuwait. Facing negligible resistance from its much smaller neighbor, Iraq's tanks stormed in blitzkrieg fashion through Kuwait in a few short hours. With more than 100,000 troops, along with tanks, artillery, and surface-to-surface missiles, Iraq now occupies Kuwait.

This aggression came just hours after Saddam Hussein specifically assured numerous countries in the area that there would be no invasion. There is no justification whatsoever for this outrageous and brutal act of aggression.

A puppet regime imposed from the outside is unacceptable. The acquisition of territory by force is unacceptable. No one, friend or foe, should doubt our desire for peace, and no one should underestimate our determination to confront aggression.

Four simple principles guide our policy. First, we seek the immediate, unconditional, and complete withdrawal of all Iraqi forces from Kuwait. Second, Kuwait's legitimate government must be restored to replace the puppet regime. And third, my administration, as has been the case with every president from President Roosevelt to President Reagan, is committed to the security and stability of the Persian Gulf. And fourth, I am determined to protect the lives of American citizens abroad.

Immediately after the Iraqi invasion, I ordered an embargo of all trade with Iraq and, together with many other nations, announced sanctions that both froze all Iraqi assets in this country and protected Kuwait's assets. The stakes are high. Iraq is already a rich and powerful country that possesses the world's second largest reserves of oil and over a million men under arms. It's the fourth largest military in the world.

Our country now imports nearly half the oil it consumes and could face a major threat to its economic independence. Much of the world is even more dependent upon imported oil and is even more vulnerable to Iraqi threats.

We succeeded in the struggle for freedom in Europe because we and our allies remained stalwart. Keeping the peace in the Middle East will require no less. We're beginning a new era. This new era can be full of promise. An age of freedom. A time of peace for all peoples. But if history teaches us anything, it is that we must resist aggression or it will destroy our freedoms. Appeasement does not work. As was the case in the 1930s, we see in Saddam Hussein an aggressive dictator threatening his neighbors. Only 14 days ago Saddam Hussein promised his friends he would not invade Kuwait. And four days ago he promised the world he would withdraw. And twice we have seen what his promises mean. His promises mean nothing.

In the last few days I've spoken with political leaders from the Middle East, Europe, Asia, and the Americas, and I've met with Prime Minister Thatcher, Prime Minister Mulroney, and NATO Secretary General Woerner. And all agree that Iraq cannot be allowed to benefit from its invasion of Kuwait.

We agree that this is not an American problem or a European problem or a Middle East problem. It is the world's problem. And that's why, soon after the Iraqi invasion, the United Nations Security Council, without dissent, condemned Iraq, calling for the immediate and unconditional withdrawal of its troops from Kuwait. The Arab world, through both the Arab League and the Gulf Cooperation council, courageously announced its opposition to Iraqi aggression. Japan, the United Kingdom, and France, and other governments around the world have imposed severe sanctions. The Soviet Union and China ended all arms sales to Iraq.

And this past Monday, the United Nations Security Council approved for the first time in 23 years mandatory sanctions under Chapter VII of the United Nations Charter. These sanctions, now enshrined in international law, have the potential to deny Iraq the fruits of aggression, while sharply limiting its ability to either import or export anything of value— especially oil.

I pledge here today that the United States will do its part to see that these sanctions are effective and to induce Iraq to withdraw without delay from Kuwait.

But we must recognize that Iraq may not stop using force to advance its ambitions. Iraq has massed an enormous war machine on the Saudi border, capable of initiating hostilities with little or no additional preparation. Given the Iraqi government's history of aggression against its own citizens as well as its neighbors, to assume Iraq will not attack again would be unwise and unrealistic.

And therefore, after consulting with King Fahd, I sent Secretary of Defense Dick Cheney to discuss cooperative measures we could take. Following those meetings the Saudi government requested our help. And I responded to that request by ordering U.S. air and ground forces to deploy to the Kingdom of Saudi Arabia.

Let me be clear. The sovereign independence of Saudi Arabia is of vital interest to the United States. This decision, which I shared with the congressional leadership, grows out of the longstanding friendship and security relationship between the United States and Saudi Arabia. U.S. forces will work together with those of Saudi Arabia and other nations to preserve the integrity of Saudi Arabia and to deter further Iraqi aggression.

Through their presence, as well as through training and exercises, these multinational forces will enhance the overall capability of Saudi armed forces to defend the Kingdom. I want to be clear about what we are doing and why. America does not seek conflict, nor do we seek to chart the destiny of other nations. But America will stand by her friends. The mission of our troops is wholly defensive. Hopefully, they will not be needed long. They will not initiate hostilities, but they will defend themselves, the Kingdom of Saudi Arabia, and other friends in the Persian Gulf.

We are working around the clock to deter Iraq aggression and to enforce U.N. sanctions. I'm continuing my conversations with world leaders. Secretary of Defense Cheney has just returned from valuable consultations with President Mubarak of Egypt and King Hassan of Morocco. Secretary of State Baker has consulted with his counterparts in many nations, including the Soviet Union. And today he heads to Europe to consult with President Ozal of Turkey, a staunch friend of the United States. And he'll then consult with the NATO foreign ministers.

I will ask oil-producing nations to do what they can to increase production in order to minimize any impact that oil flow reductions will have on the world economy. And I will explore whether we and our allies should draw down our strategic petroleum reserves. Conservation measures can also help. Americans everywhere must do their part. And one more thing. I'm asking the oil companies to do their fair share. They should show restraint and not abuse today's uncertainties to raise prices.

Standing up for our principles will not come easy. It may take time and possibly cost a great deal. But we are asking no more of anyone than of the brave young men and women of our Armed Forces and their families. And I ask that in the churches around the country prayers be said for those who are committed to protect and defend America's interests.

Standing up for our principles is an American tradition. As it has so many times before, it may take time and tremendous effort. But most of all, it will take unity of purpose.

As I've witnessed throughout my life in both war and peace, America has never wavered when her purpose is driven by principle. And on this August day, at home and abroad, I know she will do no less.

Thank you and God bless the United States of America.

ENDNOTE

1. Delivered on August 8, 1990, The White House, Washington, D.C.

CHAPTER 8
Defending the Kingdom[1]

Fahd Bin Adul Aziz

In the name of God, the Merciful, the compassionate. Thanks be to God, Master of the Universe, and Prayers of Peace be upon the last Prophets Mohamad and all his kinfolk and companions.

Dear brother citizens, may God's peace and mercy be upon you.

You realize, no doubt, through following up the course of the regrettable events in the Arab Gulf region during the last few days the gravity of the situation the Arab Nation faces in the current circumstances. You undoubtedly know that the government of the kingdom of Saudi Arabia has exerted all possible efforts with the governments of the Iraqi Republic and the state of Kuwait to contain the dispute between the two countries.

In this context, I made numerous telephone calls and held fraternal talks with the brothers. As a result, a bilateral meeting was held between the Iraqi and Kuwaiti delegations in Saudi Arabia with the aim of bridging the gap and narrowing differences to avert any further escalation.

A number of brotherly Arab kings and presidents contributed, thankfully, in these efforts based on their belief in the unity of the Arab Nation and the cohesion of its solidarity and cooperation to achieve success in serving its fateful causes.

However, regrettably enough, events took an adverse course to our endeavors and the aspirations of the peoples of the Islamic and Arab nation, as well as all peace-loving countries.

Nevertheless, these painful and regrettable events started in the predawn hours of Thursday 11 Muharram 1411H., corresponding to 2nd August A. D. 1990. They took the whole world by surprise when the Iraqi forces stormed the brotherly state of Kuwait in the most sinister aggression witnessed by the Arab nation in its modern history. Such an invasion inflicted painful suffering on the Kuwaitis and rendered them homeless.

While expressing its deep displeasure at this aggression on the brotherly neighbor Kuwait, the kingdom of Saudi Arabia declares its categorical rejection of all ensuring measures and declarations that followed that aggression, which were rejected by all the statements issued by Arab leaderships, the Arab League, the Islamic Conference Organization, and the Gulf Cooperation Council, as well as all Arab and international bodies and organizations.

The kingdom of Saudi Arabia reaffirms its demand to restore the situation in the brotherly state of Kuwait to its original status before the Iraqi storming as well as the return of the ruling family headed by H.H. Sheik Jaber al-Ahmed al-Sabah, the Emir of Kuwait, and his government.

We hope that the emergency Arab summit called by H.E. President Mohamad Hosni Mubarak of sisterly Egypt will lead to the achievement of the results that realize the aspirations of the Arab nation and bolster its march towards solidarity and unity of opinion.

In the aftermath of this regrettable event, Iraq massed huge forces on the borders of the kingdom of Saudi Arabia. In view of these bitter realities and out of the eagerness of the kingdom to safeguard its territory and protect its vital and economic potentials, and its wish to bolster its defensive capabilities and to raise the level of training of its armed forces—in addition to the keenness of the government of the kingdom to resort to peace and non-recourse to force to solve disputes—the kingdom of Saudi Arabia expressed its wish for the participation of fraternal Arab forces and other friendly forces.

Thus, the governments of the United States, Britain, and other nations took the initiative, based on the friendly relations that link the kingdom of Saudi Arabia and these countries, to dispatch air and land forces to sustain the Saudi armed forces in performing their duty to defend the homeland and the citizens against any aggression with the full emphasis that this measure is not addressed to anybody. It is merely and purely for defensive purposes, imposed by the current circumstances faced by the kingdom of Saudi Arabia.

It is worth mentioning in this context that the forces that will participate in the joint training exercises with the Saudi armed forces are of a temporary nature. They will leave the Saudi territory immediately at the request of the kingdom.

We pray to Almighty God to culminate our steps towards everything in which lie the good of our religion and safety of our homeland, and to guide us on the right path.

May God's peace and blessing be upon you.

ENDNOTE

1. Delivered on August 9, 1990, Riyadh, Saudi Arabia

PART TWO
SAUDI ARABIAN MODERIZATION

CHAPTER 9
Saudia Arabia: From Tribal Society to Nation-State

John Duke Anthony

In any discussion of economic development in Saudi Arabia, the matter of linkages to social and political variables is often raised. In the present context, this is not only natural but realistic and appropriate, serving as it does to underscore the interdependent universe in which development is proceeding. Whether one is examining five-year plans or such technically complex phenomena as absorptive capacity and industrialization, the utility of sociological perspectives would seem to be self-evident. In considering the circumstances of the people affected by the development process, some brief comments on the kingdom's basic social units—in this instance, tribes—may therefore be of value.

This focus on a traditional "interest" group is admittedly limited. It clearly highlights but one kind of voluntary association among many others involved in the development equation. Depending on perspective, there may be other limitations in this approach as well: more than a few critics who grapple with the amorphous concept of social change in Saudi Arabia, for example, consider contemporary concern with such phenomena as distinctly unmodern, if not anachronistic. Yet, in terms of examining the impact of development in the kingdom, the tribe qualifies as well as any other grouping as a useful unit of analysis.

The Tribe's Established Role

A consideration of particular relevance in this regard is the fact that tribes were the basic social and political units to which many Saudi Arabians looked for centuries for the preservation of order and the resolution of conflict. More than that, in pre-oil Arabia they were the repositories of both the means and actual process of a substantial proportion of what limited production occurred in the non-urban areas.

To be sure, the functions of maintaining order and administering justice are nowadays attended to by somewhat newer political structures associated with the central, regional, and local governments. Even so, there remain hundreds of tribes and subtribes scattered across the kingdom, as in the two Yemens and Oman. And while the numbers of tribes are not nearly as great outside those four countries, the same phenomenon persists throughout all Arabia. Indeed, despite a half century's official campaign against tribalism in the name of encouraging national and Islamic solidarity, clan and lineage links remain a potent force in Saudi Arabian society. The ongoing manifestation of such forces has long been especially pronounced in terms of the innermost circle of the ruler's entourage: the Ahl Al Sheikh, the Ahl al-'Aqd wa al-Hal, and even the Council of Ministers.

Among the most important tribes in the kingdom over the years have been the following: 'Anaza, Harb, Utaybah, Al Murrah, Shammar, Mutayr, and Qahtan, to name perhaps the seven largest in terms of members. Hardly less significant have been the Ruwala, Dawasir, Manasir, Munjaha, Yam, Ghamid, Shah Ran, Al Jahadilah, Juhaynah, Bait, Huwaytat, Bani Hajir, Bani Khalid, Quraysh, Al Rashid, 'Ajman, and Awazim. For much of Arabian history—indeed, until well into this century—most of these tribes existed as independent political entities in microcosm. As such, they were capable, like other groups (for example, the ulama or religious leaders, the merchants, and members of important families) of uniting for common action. At the same time, however, they more often than not acted as divisive forces in any larger societal context.

It was this latter characteristic as much as any other attribute that prompted the late King Abdul Aziz, founder of modern Saudi Arabia, to seek a number of means by which he could integrate the various tribes into the new national political structure of the kingdom. The religious content of Abdul Aziz's message as he set about knitting Arabia into a single state proved to be his greatest source of strength. He was able to direct and control a strict adherence to Islamic doctrines and, in this manner, affect a significant modification of the tribal distinctions that formerly had divided the realm.

Besides military conquest and spreading the discipline of the Hanbali school of Islamic law, Abdul Aziz employed to great effect one other means of unification—the institution of marriage. Through this device he was able to fuse further the interests and destinies of the tribes. In his own case, he married into many of the most important tribes and produced a far more numerous progeny than ordinarily would have been possible. Many of Adbul Aziz's numerous sons (plus more than 100 grandsons and more than 500 great-grandsons) and daughters have continued the broadening of the base of support for the ruling family by marrying, in their turn, the members of families of different tribes. As a result, it is now difficult to find major tribes in the kingdom without some close family link to the ruling household. Both his efforts and those of his successors necessitated the creative ingenuity of compromise. The accommodations produced, however, have resulted in new patterns of order in a national context.

To be sure, the compromises required and the adjustments achieved could hardly be expected to have been entirely satisfactory to either the tribal sheikhs or the country's development leaders. Yet the process itself, half a century old, is much further along than in several neighboring countries. And, as the 1980s began, there was little doubt that countrywide there had been a definite shift in the direction of public sentiments and outlook. In essence, the shift was away from the more traditional and local orientations of the past to more general affiliations.

Even so, for most of the population born before World War II, tribal affiliation has remained an important symbol identifying their membership in the wider Saudi Arabian society. Such affiliation in the contemporary era has been a significant link between a great many individuals and the regime in Riyadh, providing them with prima facie evidence of a claim to the rights, duties, and privileges of citizenship. The point is hardly an insignificant one: such documentation has frequently constituted the all-important admission ticket for the positions of employment available to Saudi Arabians. Equally, in the absence of any other form of documentation for purpose of identification, it has made possible the entrance of countless Saudi Arabians into one of the local school systems, gained them access to the government's health facilities, and, for those who sought to travel abroad, warranted the issuance of passports in their names.

Distinguishing Tribal Factors

In the early years of this century, a number of tribes proved politically decisive both to the ongoing acceptance of Al Saud rule in the Najd and, no less important, to the extension of the ruling family's writ to areas previously under different administrative control. Among the more highly regarded tribal groupings in this regard were the Qahtan, the Mutayr, Utayban, Dawasir, the Shammar, the Al Murrah and, of course the Anaza, from which the Al Saud themselves claim to originate (as do their dynastic counterparts in Bahrain and Kuwait).

The importance of these and other tribes derived more often than not from a combination of one or more of the following factors: size, military power, geographic location, form of livelihood, character and orientation of leadership and progeny, and/or religious outlook. In earlier times, another factor was often identification with one side or the other in a fundamental genealogical (not necessarily ethnic) distinction between the Adnani and Qahtani elements among the tribal population, whose roots predate the Islamic era.

That the size of a given tribe has not always been directly related to its influence, however, has been exemplified historically by the Quraysh, the tribe of the Prophet Muhammad. Several tribes are larger. Similarly, the importance of other tribes in earlier days stemmed less from their numbers than their military power and—of crucial importance in determining their influence over time—their reputation of being among the most consistently loyal to the central government. In recognition of these two traits, it is of considerable contemporary significance that members of such tribes form to this day a substantial segment among the country's National Guardsmen, headed by Emir Abdallah.

The Manasir, AI Murrah, the Shammar, the Anaza, Ruwala, and the Huwaytat, among others, have long been of special importance strategically, owing to their location near (and often extending beyond) the country's borders and to their traditional ties with neighboring states. A number of these tribesmen at times have made the conduct of relations between the Riyadh government and such states as Iraq, Kuwait, Jordan, Abu Dhabi (United Arab Emirates), and Oman much more complicated than would have been the case had they been positioned instead deep within the interior of Arabia.

Other tribes have been influential for reasons having little to do with their numbers, military prowess, or territorial position. Due to their origins, substantial segments of some tribes, for example, remain distinguished by their long-standing cultural orientation toward areas other than Riyadh: the coastal communities of the Gulf or the Red Sea in some instances, the east Arabian areas beyond the Rub' al-Khali Desert in others, and now and again one or the other of the Yemens. One tribe, the Shammar—whose members extend into Syria and as far into Iraq as Mosul—is of added significance owing to the fact that the mother of the previously mentioned Emir Abdallah, a key leader in the ruling family, was one of its more important members.

The notion of "tribe" has not in every instance involved a social or political entity. Indeed, at times some groups have been considered tribes even though they may not have been known or prone to act as a single unit. For these and other groups, the term "tribe" has become associated more and more with the idea of a loosely knit membership unit. Such groups are typically devoid of any past or present implications of sovereignty or even autonomy. Yet they manifest such unifying characteristics as ethnic homogeneity, cultural continuity, linguistic similarity, and/or a common, deep-seated attachment to a given geographical area. In the past the close identification of many tribes with the last-mentioned trait gave rise to much strife and internicine tension between neighboring tribes, causing in turn the creation of competing coalitions of tribal groupings from different descent groups.

No less affected by the changes of the past half-century have been the tribal sheikhs. The tribal sheikhs have traditionally played a role that goes far beyond merely enhancing tribal identification in the kingdom. The influence of tribal leaders for many years derived largely from their role as a major channel of communication between the authorities in Riyadh and the country's hundreds of thousands of tribesmen. Yet there were always well-defined limits to the manifestation of their influence. Whether the tribe was settled or nomadic and whether its lands were strategically important or not, their influence seldom extended beyond the geographic locus of the tribe itself.

The Family Unit in Saudi Society

Finally, with respect to all the tribes in the kingdom, it is impossible to gain an adequate picture of their social and political organization without an examination of family structure. The impact of the family as an extended unit on government has, of course, been immense in the formation of past and present political structures in Arabia. Yet its paramountcy in the initial formation of the tribes themselves has often been overlooked along with the predominant role of one or more families in the determination of the political functions expected of the tribal sheikh. Most important of all, perhaps, is the fact that tribal roles were usually the roles of a particular family writ large. This certainly appears to have been the case with respect to the Al Saud, which over time eclipsed the political role of its tribal progenitors.

As the core unit within the overall system of political activity in the kingdom, the government knows it is on firm sociological and doctrinal ground in emphasizing, as it has repeatedly done, the ongoing importance of familial solidarity as a fundamental value. In its view, the family—far more so than the tribe or other kinds of societal groupings—remains the structural foundation on which, ultimately, the edifice of the Saudi Arabian state will stand or fall. Indeed, much is made of the fact that this one unit remains at the center of the process through which the procreation and perpetuation of all the other social units in the kingdom is manifested. Of no less significance, it remains the key unit through which lineage (read individual and group identity) is maintained, social cohesiveness is reinforced and nourished, and, by extension, structural integrity up through the highest levels of national government is enhanced. By contrast, the overall degree of influence wielded by tribal leaders as a whole has been diminished considerably as a result of numerous forces of change, which they find increasingly difficult to control or influence in their favor.

Tribal Units and the Future

The growing impact of the central authority on traditional tribal autonomy and the effect of a rapidly expanding national economy continue to affect the influence of all the Kingdom's tribal leaders. The first factor has been manifested by the ambitious development programs and administrative machinery of Riyadh and the individual governates that have drawn the tribal population and its leaders ever closer into the government's orbit. The second has long been evidenced by the growing numbers of Saudi Arabian citizens migrating away from the kingdom's villages—and in the process, of course, from the authority of the tribal sheikhs—to the urban centers of Riyadh, Dhahran, Abha, Jeddah, and elsewhere, where opportunities for wage and salaried employment abound.

Although it may yet be too early to discern the ultimate impact of these phenomena on the roles of individual tribes and their sheikhs within the national political structure, there is evidence enough to indicate some of the consequences of the trend to date. There is little doubt, for example, that the previous rather marked polarity between the interior-based capital and some of the country's more remote areas—indeed, among the coastal mountainous and desert regions in general, not to mention more intricate polarities between and within these regions—has become more and more blurred with each passing year. In its place there is no question that new links between and within these areas have emerged. The tribal sheikhs, moreover, have long since been unable or unwilling to reverse this trend that has relegated more and more of them to a lower echelon within the overall political structure.

To conclude, it is clear that the process of modernizing and diversifying the economy and other sectors of national life has brought vast changes to the position and role of the kingdom's tribes. Looking to the future, the process seems certain to continue, given the government's ongoing commitment to promoting economic growth, industrialization, and numerous other changes along a broad societal front. Equally assured will be the continuing challenge to development planners, economists, and many other Saudi Arabian leaders of managing some of the basic kinds of conflict—especially those associated with psychological stress and moral unease—which often become manifest in such a process, and of working these conflicts out between the central and local authorities.

CHAPTER 10
The Transition from a Tribal Society
to a Nation-State

Abdulrahman H. Al-Said

It is perhaps useful to indicate at the outset what this chapter is not. Despite the assuming title, this chapter was not written in order to (and does not even aspire or claim to) fully trace the development of Saudi Arabia from its humble beginnings to the present times. Rather, the intent here is to put in sharper focus some of the events and developments leading to the country's emergence from a tribally organized and dominated entity to one in which authority and significant decision making are increasingly assumed by a central source of power.

Of particular interest to this effort are certain changes taking place in the various cultural, economic, and social bonds lending context and credibility to a process of national integration. Thus, in an attempt to formulate a clearer notion of Saudi Arabia's transition from an essentially tribal society to a nation-state, this chapter briefly examines the changes occurring in the following areas: (1) The decline of traditional tribal modes of existence; and (2) the process of institution building and the consolidation of authority.

Because this effort is geared toward an understanding of a transitional process, a concise delineation of its historical framework is a desirable prerequisite. For analytical purposes as well as convenience, this framework extends from the formation of the contemporary Saudi state (1932) until the end of the 1960s. This designation focuses on the dissolution of certain modes of socioeconomic organization and the appearance in their place of alternative ones. Saudi Arabia's successful unification and the country's remarkable stability is a testimony to the manner in which this transitional process has evolved. Many experts predicted a far different outcome from the one being experienced at present. D. G. Hogarth, a noted expert on the Arabian Peninsula, wrote in 1925:

> I see nothing in the circumstances or constituents of the present Wahhabite expansion to promise it a longer life than has been enjoyed by early Nejdean ebullitions. These, to take only one test, have prevailed in

Mecca for ten years, on the average . . . I prophesize, therefore, that Arabia is not in for more than a decade, at the most, of Wahhabite domination outside Nejd.[1]

Mr. Hogarth's prophecy reflected the conventional-wisdom approach of the experts. The question then becomes: What combination of forces and circumstances has altered the course of events in this part of the world? That the Arabian Peninsula and particularly Saudi Arabia have opted for an alternative mode of existence and that socioeconomic organization is the central theme of the following discussion.

Decline of Traditional Tribal Modes

Perhaps the most decisive and least understood of the transformations taking place in the Arabian Peninsula is the massive and continuous movement of people from the desert to the urban and rural centers. That this detribalization process has troubled most observers and the experts is due in no small part to the prevailing state of conceptual confusion regarding such elementary questions as, "Who can we call a Bedouin?" Unfortunately, even the "experts" have tended to perceive the Bedouins in unidimensional terms. In other words, to be Bedouin is to be totally nomadic with next to no ties to the surrounding environment. Such a view finds expression even in specialized journals and volumes such as the *Encyclopedia of Islam*, which defined the Bedouins as "pastoral nomads of Arabian blood, speech, and culture who are found in the Arabian Peninsula proper and in parts of Iran, Soviet Turkestan, North Africa, and the Sudan."[2]

This view of Bedouin life, however innocent, is as incorrect as it is unfair. The complexity of the city—desert interaction has often eluded the scholars who have dwelled on the surface manifestations of raiding, hostility, and so on—and ignored the ecological and economic underpinnings of this relationship. The scholars' attitude was undoubtedly influenced by the ideas of no less an authority than Ibn Khaldun, who conceived of the desert-town relationship as a vicious cycle of ebb and flow. But to his credit, Ibn Khaldun was speaking of a different era with a different set of circumstances. Unfortunately, this state of confusion can be detrimental to such efforts as the proper classification and enumeration of the whole populace. A clear example is provided by the 1970 United Nations Yearbook, which described the Saudi population as 85 to 95 percent Bedouin.[3] On the other hand, a recently published study suggests that as the 1980s open, perhaps 5 percent of the Saudi population remains wholly nomadic.[4] The conceptual rigidity regarding the classification of the Bedouins is undoubtedly spurred by the romantic and antiquated notion that insists on viewing them as totally nomadic and completely isolated from the sedentary population. Bedouin life, of course, has never been as static as the romanticists insist on recounting. And the demarcation line between sedentary and nomadic populations is not a hard-and-fast one.

The Transition

Central to such problems as what percent of the population can be considered Bedouin is a serious lack of understanding of the process of settlement. This process through which the Bedouins move gradually from one lifestyle into the other—often combining the two before they are absorbed into the sedentary mold—has only lately begun to receive the kind of scrutiny it deserves. Both M. Katakura, in her study of the Wadi Fatima settlements, and D. P. Cole, in his brilliant book on the Al Murrah Bedouins, provide the kind of insight needed for a proper understanding of this process.[5] Both cases, though representing different groups, document a willingness to settle in response to changing economic circumstances.

As a result of these and other lesser-known efforts, three patterns of Bedouin settlement have been identified. At the risk of oversimplification, these can be seen as: (a) nomadic Bedouins; (b) the semi-nomadic Bedouins; and (c) settled Bedouins. The first classification includes nomadic tribes—people who will "generally move around in a familiar territory," taking into consideration the state of pasture and the accessibility of a market. They live off the sale of sheep and goat fat; dried-milk cakes; sheep, goat, and camel hair; and their livestock of camels, sheep, and goats. The semi-nomadic Bedouins are half-settled communities that may eventually establish themselves in one place permanently or they may return to the nomadic life at any time. The third group of settled Bedouins lives, by and large, in huts or houses forming a village or hamlet. Some of the settled Bedouins work as agricultural laborers, others find employment in the cities, and some engage in small-scale artisan manufacturing.

Naturally, Bedouin social organization tended to change and rearrange its rules and mechanisms—and eventually some of its values—in a manner that is compatible with the adopted pattern.

In more recent times the natural ubiquity of the process of settlement has been greatly enhanced by two external factors: oil and droughts. The simultaneous occurrence of a prolonged drought (1958-1965) with the escalating position of economic predominance assumed by oil has confronted the Saudi Bedouin with an offer he cannot refuse. As it happened, the increasingly attractive pull of the urban economy was sharpened by the increasingly inhospitable state of dry pastures. Whether it was the result of settling in new towns near Aramco (Arabian American Oil Company) water wells, joining the National Guard or the army, entering the labor force of large companies, or owning taxis in the cities, the national economy's ability to absorb the tribal economy has been manifest. In a study commissioned by Aramco, the writers observed:

> Even among Bedouins, we are told, the older tribal and sub-tribal allegiances are being replaced by the idea that the center and not the tribal head or his subordinate is seen as the source of effective power and the place for submitting petitions and bringing requests. Wealth has loosened the connection between tribal leaders and the common man, and the rise of a wealthy central government has, together with this, promoted a more direct relationship between the people and the top.[6]

Institution Building and Consolidation of Authority

The erosion of the social, economic, and cultural bases of the Bedouin social system was accompanied by a similarly significant phenomenon. The emergence of strong and central institutions hailed a new era and paved the way for significant changes in all areas of national life. The cornerstone for much of this change was the Council of Ministers, which was created in the final days of King Abdul Aziz's reign (1953). Of special interest in this connection was the implicit recognition of the need to identify areas of responsibility, to separate them, and to delegate authority in accordance with a more formal set of rules and procedures. This mushrooming of governmental institutions represented an attempt to cope with a condition of "rising expectations." As the citizens heard of the building of new schools and municipalities in neighboring towns and cities, delegations would go to the capital and demand similar privileges. As a result, limited and understaffed ministries of yesterday were giving way to larger and more numerous ministries and bureaus.

The steady growth of the central government and its bureaucratic apparatus has tended to weaken local power centers in the cities and provinces. This process seems to have proceeded in two stages. First, a considerable weakening of the powers of the city "notables" greatly enhanced the role of the bureaucracy. The notables, a residue of tribal strength, were unofficial representatives of the various tribes and families residing in an area and collectively sharing in the decisions affecting the other residents. In most cases they were joined by a representative(s) of the religious establishment and occasionally by others famous for their wisdom and influence. Second, this was followed by a visible reduction and minimization of the powers and prerogatives of provincial governors (emirs). These two centers of local power were, since the inception of the Kingdom, able to retain a great deal of influence over governmental plans and projects designed for their respective areas. In the case of the notables, this power was manifested in their ability to suggest to the central government the desirability of a certain project or to point out the lack of such desirability. The central government never felt that this was more than a mere privilege to suggest, and when it deemed it necessary, its plans and projects were carried out despite the notables' objections. The governors, on the other hand, were representatives of the central authority with vast administrative and executive powers over their respective provinces.

The Transition

The decline of the notables as a viable social force was a gradual and almost invisible process. As the bureaucracy expanded and became less inclined to heed their advice and as the ranks of their elders thinned as a result of death, old age, or mere inertia, this institution faded and was relegated to perform mere ceremonial tasks. For example, in the city of Buraydah, about 470 kilometers northwest of Riyadh, the notables exhibited opposition to many government projects. In the early 1960s the government decided to establish a girls' school in Buraydah. The notables "sent a delegation 200 miles across the desert to protest. When the school was about to open, however, the townsfolk threatened to tear it down. Faisal sent armed guards to protect the school."[7] Encouraged by the King's steadfastness, another delegation representing bureaucrats and school teachers asked for and got more schools. This, according to the city's mayor, "considerably weakened the notables." A general feeling of "lack of irrelevance" to new situations developed even "among some members of the council." Councils of notables varied in terms of their significance because of, among other things, the region's particular tribal configuration. The eclipse of traditional centers of power as represented by the town notables and Bedouin sheikhs, in favor of a centralized authority, has further curbed provincial particularism and eased the transitional process.

Unlike the decline of the institution of the notables, the reduction of the governors' power was not a response to the state's need for asserting its authority nor the removal of obstacles for the implementation of its plans and projects. This was a natural outcome of the tendency to confer more power on the central government, a result in no small measure of the Council of Ministers' emergence as a viable source of authority. Ministries such as Health, Education, and Finance created provincial offices, and "these have represented a great inroad into the former sphere of authority of the local Amirate [governorship] . . . . The institution he [the governor] so long embodied has seen new functions grow up beyond its sphere of competence and old ones removed from its control."[8]

The governor, originally intended to be the personal representative of the king and his principal agent in the area, was expected to oversee and direct all governmental activity in his area of jurisdiction. The simple nature of many of the projects started between the 1930s through the 1950s did not require any significant alteration of this formula. However, the mushrooming of agencies and the explosion of the civil service in the 1960s (the government doubled the number of its employees between 1962 and 1967) radically changed this situation. At present the governor is still responsible for the preservation of public order, an area over which he exercises direct control. Overall his leadership in other spheres of government, however, has greatly diminished. Some exceptions exist. The emergence in the last few years of dynamic and technically competent governors such as Prince Khaled Al-Faisal (governor of Asir) has restored to that office a considerable degree of influence and vitality.

Thus both the decline of the institution of notables and the reduction of the governors' power ushered in an era of increased national integration and decreased fragmentation and provincialism. Measures that were originally applied to some provinces were now applied nationally. All over the country people came to look to Riyadh and to the government's budget for information regarding projects and expenditures in their area. Instead of going to the provincial governor with requests for more schools and hospitals, delegations flocked to Riyadh in order to lobby ministers and bureaucrats. This might be judged a classic case of moving from a traditional to a rational basis of authority, and in the narrow sense of the concept, such would be correct.[9]

Another significant development was taking place in the educational sphere. The establishment of a unified educational system catering to students from all parts of the kingdom was significant in at least one respect: students for the first time were reading the same curriculum and were thus being socialized along the same lines. This aspect of the socialization process represented a radical departure from that to which their parents were exposed and can be seen as a catalyst leading to the emergence of a new national consciousness. The government's extensive scholarship programs have allowed thousands of students (some of them leaving their home town for the first time) to live and study as colleagues and roommates, enabling them, at a crucial stage in their lives, to draw on shared experiences. In a land where people were identified either through their tribes or their towns and villages, the forging of a new identity superseding the old and familiar one is a matter of high priority on the road to national homogenization and nation-statehood. Professor A. Mazrul asserted the significance of this catalyst: "It can therefore be seen that a process of cultural fusion—leading to an enlarged empathy... of a shared life style—is a contribution toward the integrative process."[10]

The process of national integration has been accelerated by the revolution in communications. In this regard, the state's ability to introduce visible and significant economic changes is augmented by its access to powerful and persuasive means of communication such as radio and television. The widespread use of radio, especially, has introduced the nomad and the farmer to the larger society. Their limited picture of their milieu and their needs was changed as a result. Katakura found during her stay among the Wadi Fatima nomads and farmers that "When I asked a group of them what they might call a new settlement, they answered jokingly 'Toshiba!' for most of the villages had transistor radios."[11] Cognitive frontiers were extended, and the reluctance to be a part of a larger unit was to a considerable degree curbed and neutralized. Earlier, as is well known, isolationism and provincialism were not characteristic only of the Bedouins and farmers. In fact, the whole area was governed by a compartmentalized mentality, a result, to a large degree, of the prevailing state of geographical insulation. According to George Rentz [an authority on Saudi Arabia] previously "isolated from one another, people thought of themselves as citizens of the Hijaz or of Najd rather than of a larger entity."[12] The de facto reversal of this situation came as a result of the unification of the country in the 1930s, but its *de jure* realization came on the heels of the great changes of the 1960s. As Frank Tachau has pointed out:

> The resources which have become available to the whole provide a clear and immediate means and motive for avoiding the fragmentation into the older component parts which might leave some of these parts without sufficient resources for their own development or an increased standard of living.[13]

ENDNOTES

1. D. G. Hogarth, *The Wandering Scholar* (London and New York: H. Milford and Oxford University Press, 1925), p. 77.

2. *Encyclopedia of Islam* (Leiden: Brill Publishers, 1960), p. 872.

3. United Nations, *Yearbook of the United Nations, 1970* (New York: United Nations, 1970).

4. Fouad Al-Farsy, *Saudi Arabia: A Case Study in Development,* 2nd ed. (London: Stacey International, 1980), p. 78.

5. Motoko Katakura, *Bedouin Village* (Tokyo: University of Tokyo Press, 1977) and Donald P. Cole, *Nomads of the Nomads* (Arlington Heights, Ill.: AHM Publishing, 1975).

6. Aramco Special Study Group, Thomas O'Dea, ed., "Social Change in Saudi Arabia: Problems and Prospects," Dhahran, Arabian American Oil Company (Aramco), 1963, p. 70 (mimeographed). This unpublished report is cited in A. H. Said, "Saudi Arabia: The Transition From a Tribal Society to a Nation-State" (Ph.D. dissertation, University of Missouri, Columbia, 1979), bibliography.

7. *Reader's Digest,* January 1967, p. 118.

8. Aramco Special Study Group, "Social Change in Saudi Arabia," pp. 71-73.

9. As, for example, Max Weber, *Economic and Society: An Outline of Interpretive Sociology,* ed. Guenther Roth and Claus Wittich (New York: Bedminister Press, 1968).

10. Ali Mazrui, *Cultural Engineering and Nation-Building in East Africa* (Evanston, Ill.: Northwestern University Press, 1972), p. 278.

11. Katakura, *Bedouin Village,* p. 27.

12. George Rentz, "Saudi Arabia: The Islamic Island," in *Modernization of the Arab World,* ed. J. H. Thompson and R. C. Reischauer (Princeton, N.J.: Van Nostrand, 1966), p. 188.

13. Frank Tachau, ed., *Political Elites and Political Development in the Middle East* (Cambridge, MA: Schenkman, 1975), p. 182.

CHAPTER 11
The "Desert Democracy"
David B. Ottaway

It was shortly before noontime prayers and the main hall of the Governor's Palace in central Riyadh was lined with silent, waiting petitioners, mostly elderly Saudis dressed in traditional flowing robes and checkered headdresses.

Palace chamberlains and messengers, wearing gilt swords at the waist and leather bandoliers studded with silver bullets and bearing a pistol across the chest, scurried about on princely errands.

Suddenly, all eyes were riveted on the doorway as Prince Salman, province governor and one of the kingdom's most powerful men, entered and crossed to an antechamber, with the assembled petitioners falling behind to pray with him on Oriental rugs spread out for the occasion.

Afterward, the traditional ceremony of the *majlis* (assembly) began. As the tall prince stood solemnly beneath the picture of King Abdulaziz, founder of today's kingdom, each petitioner came up and presented his complaint. Some were scrawled on a crumpled piece of paper and barely legible; others neatly typewritten by a professional scribe. After handing them over, each kissed the prince on the right shoulder and then retreated to his seat without saying a word.

The prince sat down in his straight-backed chair to read the forty or more petitions. As he finished each one, he called out the name of the owner and dispatched him with a messenger to deal with the complaint. Once, he leaned over to discuss with a bearded old man the details of his problem.

The issues before the prince could not have been more mundane. One petitioner was asking permission to break into his apartment because the man renting it had disappeared with the key and without paying the electricity bill.

Another, a Bedouin, was asking help in getting an official deed for the land he said he owned, although he had no document to prove it.

A third needed birth certificates for his children and a fourth was asking release of his father, jailed for drunkenness.

Salman dealt with most of the petitions simply by referring them to the appropriate government ministry and writing on them the words "according to instructions" meaning those of the pertinent office.

But his stamp and personal attention apparently were enough to give hope to his suppliants that justice would be done.

In this manner a kind of desert democracy is enacted daily by the ruling House of Saud in a modern urban setting as important princes, provincial governors, and village mayors meet the people in majlises across the kingdom. Although the aging and frail King Khalid [who died in 1982] had reduced his meetings to Mondays, others, like Salman, hold two every day. The prince, 44, who has been Riyadh's governor for twenty-five years, also opens up his home after dinner for four hours on most days.

"As long as we pray and go out to meet our people, then we will be in good shape," he said in an interview. "But if you hear we have lost these two things then you know we are in trouble."

Salman freely admits that listening to his subjects' complaints is a time-consuming and tiring business. Yet the institution of the majlis is held in as much esteem by Saudi rulers as a cornerstone of their political system as Congress is by Americans.

"It comes from the tradition of King Abdelaziz and we have to keep it," explained Abdullah Sudairi, Salman's American-educated secretary. "The people believe in direct contact with their prince even if there are government offices to handle it."

"This way the prince can feel the sentiments of the people and that is one reason for the stability of the country. The shah of Iran, he didn't do it," Sudairi said.

Whether the majlis is any longer capable of a role in this complex and sophisticated but largely nondemocratic society is a question that has been under debate here for some years. The kingdom has no constitution, bill of rights, or parliament, and all decisions are made either by the royal family or the twenty-four-man Council of Ministers.

The law of the land is the Sharia, the tenets of Islam governing every aspect of life and stemming from the Koran.

Although the majlis provides communication between the rulers, educated Saudis note that one discusses weighty issues or debates state in a stylized form.

Since the time of King Abdelaziz, the monarch who by 1932 unified the kingdom through conquest of or marriage into the feuding tribes of Arabia, there has been periodic talk of establishing an appointed national shura, or consultative assembly, for such matters.

Following the attack in Mecca in November 1979, when 500 armed men occupied the Grand Mosque, Islam's holiest site, the Saudi royal family renewed its oft-stated promises to institute political reforms. Crown Prince Fahd [king since 1982], the day-to-day ruler of the kingdom, even announced that plans for a national assembly and a constitution would be drawn up in two months.

But it was not until March 1980 that a nine-man committee under Interior Minister Prince Nayif was appointed to draft the document, which was completed and submitted to King Khalid [who died in 1982] nine months later.

Since then, nothing has been heard or said publicly about its fate.

Reports say that the document includes a 200-article constitution based on Islamic law, a set of basic statutes for the government, a plan of administration for the fourteen provinces, and a definition of the powers and functions of an initially appointed national consultative assembly.

The sweeping reform that seemingly promises momentous change from family to constitutional rule does not seem to be a gripping public issue. There is nothing in the state-guided press or on government-run radio and television about it and Saudis seem uninterested when asked in private about the reform.

"They have been talking about that for twenty-five years," one Western diplomat said. "It's always imminent. We may one day be deeply shocked when and if it is established."

But the diplomat said public pressure for the reform seemed to have slacked off. "They don't need the shura as a safety valve for discontent," he said. "I think the people are too busy making money."

Some Saudis seem to feel a royally appointed assembly, probably of elders and religious leaders, is about the most that will come out of the reform and that this is hardly worth getting excited about.

"It's probably a step in the right direction," conceded one, "but it doesn't go very far."

Even when a shura does come to the kingdom, many Saudi officials believe the institution of the majlis will continue for a long time because it is the traditional Saudi way of doing business. Traditions run deep in this highly conservative kingdom.

But reporters attending Prince Salman's noontime majlis noted that virtually no young Saudis showed up to ask a favor or help. This could suggest that the younger generation at least is losing faith in the majlis of the princes and is dealing directly with the ministries instead.

Nonetheless, Salman continues to be deluged with petitioners at every session, handling on the average 100 requests a day.

"I think this tradition will last for a long time," said the prince's young secretary. "People still do want direct contact with their ruler."

CHAPTER 12
Ties with Tribal Regions[1]

Helena Cobban

Saudi Arabia: The name itself has acquired a mystique, and the figures behind it are staggering. Every second of every hour of every day, just over $3,500 flows into the kingdom's budget from oil revenues. That's more than $304 million every day, more than $100 billion every year.

Even with the most extensive development plan ever unveiled anywhere, experts estimate the kingdom will be unable to spend much more than $60 billion of this annually over the next five years—much of it on armaments.

The rest, the Saudis will reluctantly have to add to their foreign capital reserves, which already stand at well over $100 billion. Reluctantly, because that oil would be a better investment left in the ground.

But the Saudis are in a bitter catch-22: Their domination of the world oil trade is such that if they cut back production to what would be economic for them, prices would soar again, bringing them back to that persistent revenue surplus.

Who are the people having to deal with such problems? They are, primarily, the heirs of the Saudi kingdom's redoubtable founder, King Abdul-Aziz (Ibn Saud).

Abdul-Aziz was not only a master of desert warfare who within a mere quarter century took his family's forces from ignominious exile in Kuwait to ruling a vast and powerful kingdom. He also had the political ability to weld the diverse parts of his nation together, bequeathing to his son Saud in 1953 a finely tuned political instrument capable of withstanding the shocks of the oil era.

King Abdul-Aziz's principal methods were those of traditional Arabian Peninsula rulers: accessibility to the least of his (male) people, and the skillful use of tribal marriage to cement his kingdom together.

King Abdul-Aziz had forty-three sons by a variety of wives from different tribes and parts of his kingdom. For the most part, the wives would remain with their families, elevated by the honor of raising, in their father's houses, a Saudi prince. The princes thus provided key links between the central Saudi family decision-making councils and the various tribes and regions.

These days, most of Abdul-Aziz's sons are old men, or, like his first two successors to the monarchy, have already passed on. But the influence of the thirty or so survivors among them remains enormous, including Khalid bin Adbul-Aziz, the present king [died 1982], and his half-brother the Crown Prince [who succeeded him in 1982 and remains as king up to the present day (2005)]. Three others, along with a grandson, the late King Faisal's son Saud, serve in the kingdom's Council of Ministers. A total of at least thirty of King Abdul-Aziz's direct descendants serve in some way in government service.

Along with other princely descendants of the original Muhammad bin Saud, these Sauds constitute the powerful family councils that rule the kingdom created in the family name.

Key allies in Saudi control of the kingdom are the Wahhabi *ulama* (plural of *alim*, a sage). Many of the ulama are descendants of the original Muhammad Abdul-Wahhab, eighteenth-century founder of this movement for Sunni fundamentalism—more particularly, of a renowned descendant of his called simply "The Sheikh."

The group of Wahhabist *ulama* provides a vital theological sanction and guidance that the Sauds have always considered an essential backing to their own early rule. When Abdul-Aziz sought to introduce radio into his kingdom, he first made sure the ulama would bless the project as an additional means of spreading God's word. Every subsequent step toward modernization has had to have their sanction.

The ulama also act as a channel between the Saud family and the even more fundamentalist of its subjects. Internal opposition to Saudi rule can spring from many sources as the society goes through all the strains of modernization, but one of the main forms of expression it takes is extreme religious fundamentalism.

Such was the movement that rocked the kingdom in November 1979 by occupying the Grand Mosque in Mecca. After the episode, the Saud family strengthened the role of the ulama, and more conservative counselors came to dominate in Saud family decision-making. But importantly, the system has shown itself flexible enough to survive.

Donald P. Cole, professor of anthropology at the American University of Cairo, has identified some elements of the social disequilibrium brought to the kingdom by the oil wealth.

At the time when Saudi decision makers are desperately trying to keep their immigrant labor force from exceeding its present level of 1.7 million, he quotes a World Bank study projecting an unemployment figure of 8 percent among the native 1.5-million-strong Saudi labor force. These unemployed are the unskilled, many of them migrants to the booming cities of the central east-west "corridor of development," having come from the nomadic and agricultural communities outside it.

Of key importance for a regime brought to power by a confederation of Bedouin tribes is the pitiful state of the estimated 25 percent of Saudis still leading a basically nomadic pastoral life.

Cash subsidies have brought the Bedouin trucks and water-tankers to help them move and increase their flocks. But Professor Cole reports that this has been insufficient to tie them into the modern, meat-hungry economy of the cities.

The fundamentalists' influence continues to grow in Saudi Arabia as in all the city states of the Gulf. But it is not the only brake increasingly being applied on the previous rush toward Western technological development. Another factor, alarming for all the oil-rich regimes, has been the explosive growth of their foreign labor force, which now outnumbers the native population in some peninsula city-states on the fringe of Saudi Arabia.

Although it has slowed, the development rush nonetheless continues. Already, fears have been expressed that it will weaken traditional Saudi modes of government. "Today's royal children are raised by English nannies in Riyadh palaces," says one Arab sociologist. "The old links with the mother's tribal region are being eroded."

And it is what is happening to those tribal regions, away from the central corridor of development, that may yet prove decisive.

ENDNOTE

1. From the *Christian Science Monitor,* July 17, 1981, reprinted with permission.

CHAPTER 13
Saudi Economy

Douglas Martin

If this country's political leaders had to run for office, they could easily point to their record in fighting inflation.

Since 1975, when inflation was running over 35 percent, the rate has dropped three or four percentage points a year. Government spending has held steady for three years running. And economic growth has averaged 21.4 percent a year since 1975.

"What we've achieved here in this country has not been done in any part of the world," said Sheik Mohammed Aba al-Khail, the Minister of Finance and National Economy. "It is really unbelievable."

Saudi Arabia's economic policymakers have some advantages: well over $100 billion in annual oil earnings, a population roughly the size of New York City's, and an exceptionally uncomplicated economy.

The apparent success of the kingdom's policies, which one Western analyst termed "a tremendously impressive achievement," thus represents the management of plenty, rather than the more common problem of coping with scarcity.

The policy has been marked by government intervention in almost every economic area, heavy subsidies to both consumers and industry, and a restrictive monetary strategy. Government spending is more than 40 times the level of 1969, but the Saudi leadership has moderated the annual rise to about 5 percent.

Saudi experts note that fiscal policy has a particularly large impact in their county because the government, which receives oil revenues directly, accounts for 80 percent of the total economy.

Pandemonium of 1973-74
The economic policy is a direct response to the pandemonium that prevailed after oil prices quadrupled in 1973-74. "This rise in government spending accelerated development of all sectors of the economy and helped change the face of Saudi Arabia beyond recognition," according to a report by the Saudi Arabian Monetary Agency.

Overnight, construction cranes seemed to replace camels as the national mascot, and construction companies came to expect profits of 100 percent on a project. Ports were congested, housing virtually unavailable, and expensive imports, from perfumes to bulldozers, flooded in.

"There were suddenly oceans more money than the country could conceivably absorb," one American economic analyst said. Inflation surged to over 40 percent and government spending doubled annually through the mid-1970s.

The Push to Relieve Inflation

After vigorous internal debate, "the government undertook an immediate crash program to alleviate inflationary pressure," a top Saudi economic official said.

One of the principal elements was to attack the bottlenecks that seemed to be contributing to inflation. Ports were expended, industrial facilities were rushed to completion, and, most importantly, tens of thousands of foreign laborers were brought to sparsely populated Saudi Arabia.

Although political analysts have suggested that the sweeping influx of foreigners, estimated at more 1.5 million people, could undermine Saudi Arabia's traditional society, economic officials tend to see the expatriates as a blessing.

"From the beginning of our program, we have benefited from the flow of foreign labor," Mr. Aba al-Khail said, in part because foreign labor is less expensive than Saudi workers.

At the same time, the government limited expenditures to an annual rate of growth considerably below the inflation rate. This curb came after three years during which public outlays had essentially doubled annually.

Subsidies to Attack Inflation

Saudi Arabia also attacked inflation with vast subsidies. As a result, food, electricity, and water all sell at a fraction—often about half—of the real cost, and medical care is free.

Another subsidy provides university students with allowances of $300 a month in addition to free tuition, books, and room and board.

Perhaps more significantly, the government began lending money in the form of twenty-five-year interest-free loans to purchase homes, a policy that also was intended to distribute some of the country's huge oil revenues. In the five years of the program, $43.7 million has been lent to built 200,000 housing units.

The great improvement in the country's inflation rate obviously owes much to these subsidies, which some analysts characterize simply as a means for Saudi Arabia to buy its way out of economic difficulties. Nonetheless, analysts do not dispute that Saudi Arabia seems to have gotten inflation under control.

Strong Monetary Assets

Saudi Arabia has monetary assets to back 100 percent of its currency in circulation, compared with a ratio as small as 10 percent in some Western nations. This buildup of assets, of course, has followed deliberate decisions not to use the assets to promote growth.

Indeed, Saudi economic authorities say that the major concern at the moment is to moderate growth, although such multibillion-dollar government efforts as the new industrial cities of Jubail and Yanbu seem crucial as Saudi Arabia's modernization continues to race ahead.

Officials say that the government's financial surplus, the excess of income over expenditure, totaled more than $30 billion in 1981. In addition, Saudi Arabia's financial reserves rose to $27 billion from $23 billion a year earlier.

Partly because of its hefty surplus, Saudi Arabian officials seem to welcome the prospect that the country's oil production this year may be reduced to support the $34-per-barrel base price set for 1982 by the Organization of Petroleum Exporting Countries. Such a move, they say, would prolong oil reserves and reduce both internal and foreign financial demands on Saudi Arabia.

Assuming a Cut in Oil Output

"Politicians tend to spend more money if they get more money," one high-placed Saudi official observed. He said that Saudi Arabia based its economic plans on an assumption of an average of 7.5 million barrels or less of daily oil production this year.

Sheik Ahmed Zaki Yamani, the oil minister, recently said that Saudi Arabia could meet all of its financial requirement with 6.2 million barrels a day of oil production. Current output is thought to be between 8 million and 8.5 million barrels daily.

On balance, Saudi Arabia's economic policymakers believe the country's program has been successful in stemming inflation, curbing the gold rush mentality that once prevailed and setting the stage for expansion of the economy beyond petroleum. "People are shifted from speculation in industry and agriculture," Sheik Soliman A. Solaim, the Commerce Minister, said. "In the years to come, we will see a maturing of the economy."

CHAPTER 14
Yanbu, a New City

Douglas Martin

This picturesque port city—with its bustling bazaar, 300-year-old coral houses and elderly men smoking strong Oriental tobacco from tableside water pipes in cafes—harkens to the fabled Arabian past.

Winding desert caravans for centuries pitched goatskin tents along Incense Road at Yanbu. Hundreds of thousands of Moslem pilgrims have passed through on their once-in-a-lifetime hajj to the holy cities of Mecca and Medina. Ancient Arab fishing dhows to this day ply the cobalt-blue waters of the Red Sea.

More and more, however, Yanbu can be viewed as a principal emblem of Saudi Arabia's future. Billions upon billions of dollars—from such huge United States companies as the Mobil Corporation—are being poured into building a huge new industrial city five miles south of the old city. Enough earth has already been moved to build twenty-three of Egypt's great pyramids. Some 30,000 people now live where there was only barren desert four years ago. More than 120,000 are expected to join them over the next quarter century.

In every direction, Saudis can be seen perched atop bulldozers instead of the camels many only recently abandoned, as they scramble to complete what is intended to be one of the world's leading refining, petrochemical, and manufacturing complexes. To Western analysts and the Saudis themselves, both the scope and intensity of the enterprise strongly suggest that the desert kingdom—holder of more than a quarter of the world's known oil reserves and the largest exporter of oil—will hardly be content to sit back while collecting hundreds of millions of dollars from its oil sales.

"We are no longer afraid of getting our hands dirty," said Yousif Ibrahim Alturki, director general of the project.

Yanbu—like Jubail, its equally brash, equally new sister city of Arabia's east coast—is intended to help satisfy some of this kingdom's deepest yearning. Before it runs out of oil or the rest of the world discovers substitute forms of energy, Saudi Arabia is fervently committed to joining the first ranks of industrial powers. The prevailing wisdom, therefore, is that a riyal spent on technology and expertise is, at the least, a riyal earned.

After years of exporting crude oil only to watch others profit handsomely by transforming it into more expensive petroleum products such as gasoline, chemicals, and plastics, Saudi Arabia is striving for a slice of this downstream action. The kingdom also is exceptionally eager to stop flaring natural gas produced with crude oil pumped for export, a practice that has obviated nocturnal darkness in the Arabian oil fields for forty years. The new plants at Yanbu and Jubail provide a sure market for this gas.

What is more, Saudi planners envision that hydrocarbon-based industries will fuel the emergence of basic industries like steel and lighter ones like consumer products, and, in the process, spawn a new class of Saudi entrepreneurs. Already, some 35 businesses—ranging from metal fabrication firms to air-conditioning installers—have permission to set up shop in an adjacent industrial park.

The lifelines of the Yanbu project are two 750-mile pipelines from Abqaiq, a town in the center of Saudi Arabia's oil fields in the eastern province on the Arabian Gulf. One is already bringing oil to Yanbu's crude oil export terminal and will supply four separate refineries within four years. The other will soon transport natural gas liquids for use as a fuel and for petrochemical feed stocks at facilities being built. Other plants are being contemplated to process and ship what are considered enormous amounts of gold, silver, zinc, and other minerals located under and near the Red Sea.

For the Western nations, analysts reason that the Yanbu development is beneficial because the use of the gas will add ten percent to the amount of Saudi Arabia's hydrocarbon reserves, thus augmenting the world's energy supplies by the equivalent of seventeen billion barrels of oil. In addition, Saudi Arabia is being further integrated into the sophisticated industrialized economies through Yanbu, Jubail, and similar efforts, thereby strengthening its already firm economic and political ties with the West.

Nonetheless, there are worries that Yanbu and other such projects could damage Western refiners and petrochemical producers because they will use natural gas priced at about fifty cents a thousand cubic feet, one-fifth the regulated United States average price and less than one-eighth the world market price. In addition, Yanbu's operations are based on the most desirable light Arabian crude, an indication that American companies may soon have to increase purchases of heavier and medium crudes if they want to maintain the same volumes of purchases. Further, there is a lingering worry that Saudi Arabia could afford to subsidize its petrochemical exports if competition significantly tightens on the world market.

For their part, Saudi planners roundly reject such worries as unjustified and unfair. "We are not threatening anybody," Sheik Alturki said. "If this is supposed to be a threat, other nations have been threatening us for the past forty years."

If the Saudis are successful—and so far they are slightly ahead of schedule—the gains will not have come easily. Unlike Jubail, there was no port, electricity, or fresh water when surveyors arrived here in 1977. Months would elapse before needed supplies arrived for the Gulf Coast of the United States and Japan. The approximately 1,500 current Saudi employees and 28,500 foreign workers and managers all had to be imported.

"It was like a commando raid," an American engineer observed with only slight exaggeration. "Four years ago, some guys waded ashore with a pick and shovel, and everything has grown from there."

Clearly, the physical challenge would have been enough, but that was only the beginning. The major obstacle has been cultural. The basis of Saudi society is a strict adherence of a fundamentalist interpretation of Islam, brooking no public places of worship for other religions, alcoholic beverages, or women in short skirts.

Thus, the coming of Western managers and Asian and African workers represents "a strain on the fabric of our culture," in Sheik Alturki's phrase. Nevertheless, he and other authorities early on decided to mix the more than forty nationalities at Yanbu to an extraordinary degree in this country of walled villas and veiled women, partly on the theory that it would be impossible to isolate the Saudis and partly in the belief that different nationalities could gain from one another.

"We are like the U.N. here," remarked Maiemona al-Dabbagh, the wife of a high-placed Saudi official, as she sipped morning coffee with several American friends. "Every day, we seem to learn something new."

The other relatively unparalleled challenge has been the manner in which Saudis have gone about development, particularly at Yanbu and Jubail. Other societies have spent years building up lighter, labor-intensive industries as a seemingly sensible prelude to emulating Pittsburgh or Houston, but this oil-blessed kingdom feels it has no such luxury, for three reasons: the cessation of gas flaring was considered an urgent step; the kingdom's population of eight to nine million tightly limits labor availability, making capital-intensive projects immediately attractive; and the government is trying to quickly channel its overflowing oil revenues into productive uses.

"To run Yanbu is a giant leap without first moving up from textile manufacturing and the like," a Western diplomat said.

The idea of a pipeline to a west coast hydrocarbon project percolated throughout the mid-1970s, as the concept of a trans-Arabian pipeline gained more and more credence. Not only is the western port 3,800 miles closer than Jubail or the kingdom's principal crude loading terminal at Ras Tanura to the major European markets, it would also help reduce Saudi Arabia's troubled reliance on the sometimes tumultuous Arabian Gulf.

Additionally, the project is viewed by some as a political sop to the economically weaker western province. Analysts suggest there might have been a particularly keen desire to aid the area, since it was originally part of the Hashemite Empire, a traditional foe of the House of Saud. The Saud family, which has ruled the gulf of the Arabian Peninsula for half a century, has developed a skill in passing out political favors that might do a Chicago ward heeler proud, according to Western analysts.

Politics, however, have been deliberately minimized in the construction and maintenance of Jubail and Yanbu. A special royal commission has been established to cut through the red tape that plagues more established bureaucracies and to diminish outside efforts to influence contracting and other big expenditures involved. Once the projects are complete, estimated around 2006, the national and local bureaucracies will resume their normal roles. For now, though, two California engineering contractors—Parsons for Yanbu and Bechtel—are providing the lion's share of ideas and planning. (Parsons' Saudi venture is half owned by the well-known Saudi businessman, Ghaith Pharaon.)

A drive around Yanbu provokes a series of insights. At night, the project's gleaming lights—strewn on tens of thousands of pieces of steel pipe—stretch across the desert like a necklace of silver and gold. There are the just-completed natural gas liquids plants, Yanbu's largest complex, which will split liquified natural gas into fuel and other components, which a $2.4-billion petrochemical plant being built by Mobil and the Saudi government will convert into valuable chemicals.

At the pristinely clean crude oil loading berth, the Washington Enterprise—a ship with an American name, a German crew, and a Liberian flag—is lifting oil at the rate of 13,000 barrels an hour. The domestic refinery that ultimately may produce as many as 400,000 barrels of oil a day for Saudi Arabia's surging gasoline market is almost complete. A $2-billion export refinery, two lubricating oil refineries, a sea water desalination plant, and an electrical generation plant also are rising from the desert.

Yanbu differs from Jubail in that it is projected to be a third to half Jubail's size and will concentrate almost exclusively on hydrocarbon-based industries. Jubail will be the home of giant steel and aluminum plants.

The projects, however, share a key characteristic: They are trying to complete quickly some of the largest-scaled construction presently being undertaken on this planet, at the same time they are creating completely new large communities. Simultaneously, Saudis—about 80 percent of whom are illiterate—must be educated to manage and operate thousands of highly sophisticated processes.

The final royal *ukase,* however, is what makes things difficult: Everything must happen at the same time. "To start with sand-and-rock desert and build a fully complete modern city in ten years is a pretty slick trick," Frederick R. Worthenn, Parsons' director of construction, said.

The Immigrant Workers in Yanbu

The 23,000 or so foreign laborers who work in Yanbu are housed in dormitories with four double-deck bunk beds along the walls. Pictures of lush Asian landscapes and Asian beauties decorate the walls. Ethnic cuisines are served in the various mess halls.

Every day it is certainly possible to eat something new. More than 100 pounds of *kim chee,* the pungent Oriental cabbage dish, is prepared for Korean workers; vats of curry are concocted for Pakistanis and Indians; fiery Thai food is available; and Arab cuisine, of course, is everywhere.

For the most part, workers say they are happy with their lot. "If I worked ten years in Sri Lanka, I couldn't make what I save here in a year," said Gamini Perera, a commissary clerk whose annual wages in Sri Lanka totaled 1,200 rupees, while in Saudi Arabia he makes the equivalent of 9,000 rupees. He adds that his yearly food and lodging, which are free to him, are worth an additional 6,000 rupees. A Filipino, Blenvenido Selvans, said his yearly earning had more than quadrupled.

The apparent satisfaction foreigners feel over their income—which sometimes supports extended families of twenty or more back home—is apparent in the quality of their work. A control center of the crude oil pipeline is so stoutly built, for instance, that experts believe it could withstand a severe bombing.

"The Koreans built it like it was on the 39th Parallel," said Lucio A. Noto, president of Mobil Saudi Arabia, Inc.

Recreational amenities are ample. Residents can swim in forty-four pools, play in the community orchestra, or check out videotapes of *Love Boat* episodes from the town library. At a soccer match the other night, Saudis, Koreans, Filipinos, and British people mixed freely. To his jeering companions, Falatah Dater, a Saudi who captains the Aramco Rising Stars, loudly boasted, "Come see us—we will take the cup."

Planners are hoping that a growing sense of community involvement will foster a municipal identity—different, of course, from the bustling bazaar quality of Jidda or the solid Saudi stability of Riyadh—but responsive to a new generation of Saudis.

CHAPTER 15
Saudi Agriculture

David B. Ottaway

This kingdom known for deserts and oil is plowing export earnings into a fertile new field—farming—with the goal of creating vast new acreage to supply the country with grain and dairy products. Saudi Arabia hopes to achieve self-sufficiency in wheat by 1986.

Tycoons with extra millions on their hands are regarded as highly patriotic to take up agriculture, and government subsidies help produce handsome returns.

The latest boom—after oil, construction, and industry—is more precisely agribusiness. Like everything in this land of vast wealth and vision, it is being done on a grand scale.

Poultry and dairy farms are sprouting like date palms around Riyadh, and on the plains, 140 miles to the east, the desert is blooming.

Spider-like wheeled, pivoted irrigation systems circle the sun-baked earth. Huge tracts of green-tipped winter wheat and forage grasses sprout. Well-digging machinery and stakes marking out new farms also are part of the new landscape.

According to Abdul Rahman Kanhal, the manager of the Harad Agricultural and Animal Production Co., the upsurge began two years ago.

"We were the first here in this region to introduce irrigation and mechanized agriculture," said Kanhal, 32, who in his long, creaseless white robe and red-checkered headdress is not exactly what one imagines of a Third World farmer. "The others saw how we did it and then started up."

Kahnal is rather typical, though, of the new Saudi farmer. The son of a vegetable and date-palm grower, he went off for a master's degree in agriculture from the University of Colorado and worked on a Colorado farm for a while.

When he came back, the only job for him was as a bureaucrat in the Agriculture Ministry. After four years he came here. Now, Saudis with agricultural degrees are a hot commodity on the tight labor market.

Kanhal manages a 10,600-acre farm, soon to be expanded to 14,400 acres, that grows wheat, peanuts, potatoes and forage grasses. It also supports 500 dairy cattle imported from

Texas and 2,000 local sheep.

The way Kanhal explains the origins of the Saudi farming boom, it combined generous government help and rich Saudi businessmen looking for good investments. "The idea is to get the sector going and then the government will withdraw," he said.

Government incentives include free land, interest-free loans up to about $5.9 million, farm equipment subsidized from thirty-five to fifty percent, fertilizer sold at half the cost, and prices guaranteed high above world market levels.

Locally grown wheat brings $1,000 a ton, compared to $300 on the world market. Milk sells at wholesale for $5.50 a gallon, four times the price in the United States.

The government Grain Silos and Flour Mill Corp. stores, mills, and markets the wheat.

"There is no problem of marketing," says Kanhal. The state-run silos "just give me a check for whatever I bring in."

Crown Prince Fahd [who has been king since 1982], the kingdom's day-to-day ruler, has just approved a $74-million investment in additional silos around Riyadh and in the Qasim regions, 500 miles to the north of the capital, to accommodate the sharp increase in wheat production.

Wheat is a high-priority item. Last year, Saudi farmers met thirty to forty percent of the country's needs, and Kahnal estimates they will double production this year. The way Saudis are opening new land, they may reach the goal of producing all they need by 1985. [Editor's note: This was the author's estimate in 1981. To see current figures, look in Part Four, "Saudi Government Documents," Chapter 31.]

Although outsiders think of Saudi Arabia as typified by the endless desert of the Rub al Khali, or Empty Quarter, there are many regions suitable for agriculture, particularly in the mountainous southern Asir Province, on the plains around Kharj and Harad, in Qasim Province, and in the world's largest oasis, Al Hasa, 100 miles north of here.

Only 1.3 million of the kingdom's 640 million acres are now devoted to farmland, with less than one quarter of that irrigated. But the government estimates the total cultivatable land at three to four times this amount and has marked out territory in each of the kingdom's thirteen provinces for new farms.

The government also has set aside $1.47 billion for loans and $735 million in subsidies to private farms during the five-year development plan that began last year. Government statistics show more than 100,000 loans made during the five years of the preceding plan.

The farm that is now the Harad Agricultural and Production Co. began fifteen years ago as a government-sponsored Bedouin settlement scheme. But as Kanhal explains it, "They all left and went to the city or into their own business."

Three years ago, the government gave more than seventy-five percent of the project to three private owners. When the farms grossed $10 million on wheat alone the first year, pressure grew on the government to turn it into a publicly owned company.

In June 1981, a National Agricultural Development Co. was created, with 2.8 million shares. The public buys shares from banks because there is no stock market. The government still holds a 20 percent interest.

Kanhal said the company is the kingdom's largest, with the main working farm here and new ones coming next year in Wadi Dawassir in the south and Hail in the north. Others are being planned.

One problem for farming, like every other activity in the kingdom, is labor. Of the 130 to 140 employees on the farm, seventy are Saudi nationals. The others include Filipinos and Sudanese. Saudi Arabia, which is one fourth as large as the United States, has a population of 8.5 million. [Editor's note: In 2004, the Saudi population was estimated at 24 million.]

"We have to be highly mechanized and don't count on casual laborers," said Kahnal.

Water is not a problem here. The farm, which sits on one of the kingdom's untapped reservoirs of oil, also has a huge underground lake. For fifteen years, the lake has provided all the water needed for irrigation, recharged by rain.

The farm's two fifteen-megawatt generators are fueled by flared gas from the oil field. The gas is provided free by the national oil company, Aramco.

CHAPTER 16
Saudi Education

Joy Winkie Viola

He is male, in his mid-20s, university-educated, deeply religious, and highly nationalistic. He is likely to be from a low- to middle-income family background. His name is Abdul. He is Saudi Arabian, and as such he is one of today's most highly sought-after human resources.

This is a profile of the average Saudi student enrolled in an American college or university. When he concludes his U.S. study program, Abdul will have his choice of career opportunities. He is inclined to want to work for the Saudi government, out of what he will say is a deep commitment to the development of his country. He is unlikely ever to become a statistic in the Third-World brain drain.

As the time of his graduation draws near, he will be courted by American multinational companies operating in Saudi Arabia, for he is their answer to "Saudization."

Who is this traveler from the Land of Black Gold? Why is he here? Why do we care?

Saudi Arabia has become a nation of significant political and economic importance to the world at large and to the U.S. in particular. It is the "boomtown" of the industrial frontier.

At present it's a maze of pipelines, power lines, bulldozers, jetties, and computers, and the site of whole new cities such as Jubail—the largest engineering endeavor in the world.

And yet, in the words of the Saudi oil minister, Sheikh Ahmad Zaki Yamani, Saudi Arabia is not a rich country. It is poor, because it lacks human resources. Nearly a million expatriates are needed in Saudi Arabia to man the industrial machine. Hence the Saudi student is in the U.S. to gain the technical, political, and economic know-how his country requires to free itself of foreign dependency and to become the master of its own destiny.

In 1948, an estimated ninety percent of the population was composed of nomads or peasant farmers and fewer than 20,000 students were enrolled in all levels of education. Today there are nearly that many Saudis enrolled in U.S. colleges and universities alone, and the total student population in the kingdom is estimated to be about 1.5 million.

U.S. participation in Saudi schooling and training has been extensive. In addition to the thousands of government and privately sponsored Saudi students enrolled in U.S. degree programs, many more are participating in manpower development programs administered by the U.S.-Saudi Arabian Joint Commission on Economic Cooperation.

Still others are participants in contractual training agreements between the Saudi government and U.S. corporations themselves. This trend is likely to continue because it is already obvious that American corporations and educational institutions will be heavily involved in the education and training required to carry out the plans of the Royal Commission for the new cities of Jubail and Yanbu.

The Saudi government appears mindful of its manpower deficiencies. Since the start of the government's three five-year development plans in 1970, the number of schools has tripled, from 2,047 to 6,641, and enrollments have risen from 589,500 to 1.5 million. Nevertheless, an estimated 80 percent of the Saudi population is still illiterate.

Whereas the first and second five-year plans stressed expansion in every phase of the economy, the third (1980-85) stresses the development of human resources needed to man that infrastructure, and to that end has authorized $52.7 billion for spending on education and training, 18.5 percent of the total budget.

Although the third still calls for across-the-board increases in educational facilities, staff, and enrollments, it also covers specific problems. Technical and vocational education will receive considerable emphasis in the face of critical deficiencies in the number of skilled indigenous personnel.

Because the education of girls continues to lag behind that of boys at all levels, new emphasis will be given to the education of women, in those fields where present cultural and religious norms permit their employment and in new career fields as well.

The role of women will continue to be dictated, however, by the strict Saudi interpretations of Islamic law, which includes the stipulation that men and women do not work together.

In higher education, efforts will be made to direct students away from traditional studies in the arts and humanities into high-priority degree programs in engineering and science and to new specializations within such fields as computer science, alternative energy sources, and telecommunications.

Finally, the government has declared an "urgent priority" to promote literacy programs among unskilled or semiskilled men aged 18 to 45 so that they can be trained in a variety of needed skills. Women, however, were excluded from this specific priority.

Although the government's commitment to education is commendable and the recent accomplishment noteworthy, many of the key problems to be addressed cannot be solved by throwing money at them. Attitudes, traditions, personal priorities, and the law of supply and demand often work at cross-purposes to the development of human resources called for in the five-year plans.

Saudi Arabia needs both plumbers and Ph.D.'s. At present, there are enough of neither, and government and industry are competing for the few that do exist. Pirating of personnel is becoming increasingly common as public and private sectors alike seek to replace expatriates with Saudi staff.

Pressure for Saudization is forcing American and other foreign companies to develop elaborate recruiting and training programs as a means of fulfilling Saudi "affirmative action." But enticing salaries and training opportunities are not always enough. Saudis are a unique people, and their motivations and values are a product of their cultural and religious traditions.

Saudis are not inclined to pursue vocational training, despite the need for skilled tradesmen and the government's establishment of numerous vocational education centers. The need for such craftsmen is so critical, however, that one American company is teaching craft skills to illiterate Saudis who lack other means of economic advancement.

Given the kingdom's ambitious development plans, however, it seems improbable that the trades will be "Saudized" for many years to come. There simply will not be enough vocationally trained Saudis to replace the present expatriate labor force.

There are similar problems at the other end of the labor scale, too. Representatives of the private sector report that the salary expectations of young college-educated Saudis are high and they are likely to expect supervisory positions. But these expectations are not necessarily unrealistic, given the limited numbers of Saudis available. Within the Saudi government, salaries are lower, but new graduates are often placed in positions of extraordinary responsibility, handling huge budgets.

In financial terms, it is a "seller's market," and a seller's market in a setting where Saudi values take precedence. The result is often one of cross-cultural conflict.

American corporate representatives express frustration over the fact that the "American work ethic," for example, is an anomaly in Saudi culture, in which great importance is placed on leisure time for family affairs and religious observances—often during the normal workday. But Saudi Arabia's emergence into the league of industrialized nations is an economic phenomenon that cannot be ignored.

That is why Abdul is so important and why young men like him will continue to remain one of the world's most sought-after human resources.

CHAPTER 17
Saudi Employment

Warren Richey

[Editor's note: Compare the economic and employment figures in this article, written in the early 1980s, to the most recent government figures given in Chapters 27 through 32 in Part Four of this book. For example, in 1981 there were two jobs available for every Saudi citizen able to fill them. In 2005, unemployment, according to the *Time Almanac,* is 25 percent. This article again reveals the difficulties of projecting current situations into the future. Just as many pundits might try to project today's situation in Saudi Arabia into the future, let this chapter show why such projections should be taken with a grain of salt.]

For every two jobs in Saudi Arabia there is one Saudi Arab available to fill them. Reducing that margin presents one of the kingdom's most serious development challenges in the 1980s.

Fueled by enormous infrastructure and industrial diversification plans funded from welling reserves of petrodollars, business is booming throughout the oil-rich kingdom.

Inherent in the boom is a commitment by government, business, and industry to create a Saudi work force capable of leading a nation whose grandfathers were Bedouin sheep herders into the ranks of the industrial world.

The plan is to achieve the "Saudization" of sectors of the economy historically dominated by foreign expertise, management, and labor. This is to be done through education and job-training programs, and by incorporating Saudi nationals into all levels of every company operating here until they make up 75 percent of each company's workforce.

The intent is to utilize fully the workforce of a country where now only 15 percent of the population is literate—much as the kingdom's planned industrial network of gas-powered generators, petrochemical complexes, and refineries is intended to maximize the utility of a single barrel of crude oil.

The difficulty, however, in establishing full Saudization of existing operations and completion of facilities under construction or still on the drawing board is that the number of new jobs is apparently growing faster than the number of Saudis who will be entering the workforce in the next five years.

At present there are 2.5 million jobs in the Saudi job market, and it is estimated that 1.1 to 1.7 million expatriates are working in the country. The exact expatriate population is a well-kept secret, but it is estimated that this population includes 800,000 from Yemen; 350,000 from other Arab countries including Palestinians; 140,000 from the Philippines, Sri Lanka, and Bangladesh; 100,000 from India and Pakistan; 80,000 from South Korea; 45,000 from America; 30,000 from the United Kingdom; and about 15,000 from Western Europe.

The total Saudi population has been estimated at 5.5 million. Between 300,000 and 700,00 new jobs are expected in the period between 1980 and 1985. During that time, 129,000 Saudi men are expected to enter the workforce.

Even considering a migration of foreign workers into Saudi Arabia and the government-forecasted shift of up to 155,000 Saudis from agriculture and construction into the new job sectors, some observers here are projecting a significant shortfall in manpower during the present five-year development plan and beyond.

The shortfall is expected by observers to lead to greater competition among major employers, who may soon be scrambling to attract employees from a limited pool of acceptable citizens to satisfy required Saudization programs. In addition, the government may have to rethink the stated policy in its "third development plan" of limiting the growth of the expatriate labor force to 9,000 during the five-year period.

Independent sources suggest that if Fiyadh attempts to limit the amount of expatriate growth by keeping it to about 1 million (as is called for in the third plan), it will cause a decline in the kingdom's growth rate, and delay—perhaps by decades—the emergence of Saudi Arabia by the year 2000 as a modern, manufacturing-oriented economy.

Part of the government's hope of keeping the number of new jobs down was based on achieving a 27.2 percent increase in productivity during the five years as workers shift to modern, capital-intensive production methods. This is expected to save the economy 700,000 jobs. Nonetheless, it appears to some that the government's two major development goals—Saudization of the work force and rapid modernization of the economy—are on a collision course.

One independent survey suggests that if the Saudis pursue development while continuing to increase the expatriate population, the relative proportion of foreigners will not begin to decline until the year 2015. In addition, the study projected that total Saudization will not occur for another seventy years.

An additional obstacle to rapid Saudization is the disparity in the distribution of foreign workers who in 1979 made up more than 75 percent of the work force in the industrial-commercial sector, the sector where most of the development is taking place. It will be especially challenging to reverse the 3-to-1 foreign-to-Saudi worker ratio in that sector, because the analysts expect that sector will swell to four million workers by the year 2000.

The Saudi government, conscious of the situation, has invested heavily in capital-intensive, highly automated plant facilities for its planned steel, fertilizer, petrochemical, and petroleum-products industries under construction at Yanbu on the Red Sea and Jubail on the Gulf. The facilities, expected to establish an industrial base from which a new manufacturing sector will blossom, will require 12,000 to 13,000 workers, according to government officials.

Officials say that they want 65 to 70 percent of the workers to be Saudi at the time the plants come on stream in the mid-1980s.

In an effort to meet this deadline, the government is matching its heavy investment in capital-intensive equipment with equally heavy investment in training and manpower development.

The government appropriated $7.83 billion of its $88.9-billion 1981-82 national budget for education and manpower. Approximately $6.75 billion was earmarked for manpower development in last year's budget.

According to the latest budget, some of the funds will be used to construct 600 schools, twenty-six intermediate colleges, eighteen health units, sixtten public libraries, twenty-six education administration buildings, and eight student sports complexes.

Some government officials expect that the government's emphasis on education will eventually allow it to tap into a pool of 100,000 students at government literacy schools.

Another aspect of the Saudi manpower shortage is that, according to custom, few Saudi women (approximately 6 percent) hold jobs, and those who do work are extremely limited in the kinds of jobs they are permitted to take.

Young Saudi males, on the other hand, particularly those with good high school grades, have become increasingly valuable assets to companies and can select from a wide range of careers. Some will choose to stay in very lucrative family businesses.

In an effort to attract educated Saudis, the Arabian American oil Company (Aramco) offers generous wage and benefit packages, plus extras like a program in which high school graduates with good grades who join the firm will be eligible for a full scholarship and salary to attend an American university after completing a three-month training course in Dhahran. In addition, Aramco, which produces 97 percent of the kingdom's oil, maintains a career development department that monitors the advancement of Saudis and assists and encourages rapid promotions.

This year approximately half of Aramco's 59,000 workers are Saudis. Aramco executives expect that its workforce will remain approximately 50 percent Saudi, assuming the firm is able to hire the equivalent of 22 percent of all Saudi males entering the job market during the present five-year plan. From 1975 to 1980 Aramco hired 15 percent of Saudis entering the labor force, competing primarily with the government for Saudi workers.

In 1981 Aramco and the government will find themselves still facing new competition for workers.

Aramco also is planning to step up its advertising campaign and to open recruiting offices throughout the nation rather than just in the oil-rich Eastern Province. It also is rapidly expanding its training programs and facilities to accommodate 21,200 newly hired Saudi trainees and Saudis switching careers by 1982.

As the kingdom's industrial sector emerges from its infancy and the oil and government sectors continue to grow, it appears that Saudi unemployment lines may be even scarcer than water in Saudi Arabia.

CHAPTER 18
Saudi Women

May-lee Chai

When I first visited Riyadh in 1975, the capital of Saudi Arabia was still more a village than a city in the modern sense. The buildings were, for the most part, low to the ground and constructed of the same adobe sand that had been used to build Arab houses for centuries. While my father, a professor, was taken to lecture at various universities, I was confined to our hotel with my mother and younger brother. Occasionally we were taken on tours with another American woman, an interior designer who had accompanied her husband, an architect, to the kingdom.

I remember traipsing through the narrow, maze-like markets where women, dressed head-to-toe in black, bought gold in great quantities: bracelets, necklaces, pendants. Everywhere. these tiny stalls were selling gold, gold, gold! The Saudis had only recently, since 1973, come into their wealth, and it seemed the women were taking no chances and investing while they could, lifting their veils momentarily to bite a coin to test its authenticity. Men in white robes and red-and-white checkered headdresses sat on piles of carpets they were trying to sell, occasionally calling out to pedestrians, before returning to their conversations with their stall mates.

The market streets were paved with cobblestones, and I remember the heat, even in December, as being oppressive. But mostly, we stayed in our hotel and watched the two channels of television, both in Arabic, which consisted largely of men in headdresses reading the news or intoning prayers from the Koran. I must have read the only book I'd brought with me from the States, *Julie of the Wolves,* a half dozen times in the three weeks of our visit.

Nearly thirty years later, on a return visit to Riyadh in June of 2003, I found the capital transformed. The change came not only because of the Al-Qaeda terrorist attack three weeks before my arrival had caused road blocks to be installed in front of every Western hotel and government building as well as in the middle of the new, American-style highways that now encircled the city.

This time, it was not just my father who was coming to lecture at universities, but me as well. I would be visiting the two most prestigious universities for women in the country, and rather than staying put in the hotel, I would be meeting and interviewing Saudi professional women and students.

As our hosts drove us from the airport into the city, I was struck by the changes that had occurred here in the span of one generation. Not only were there skyscrapers, fancy malls, and neon lights, where once upon a time the night sky even in the city had been so dark as to make the stars seem close enough to touch, but now the signs of the global economy were everywhere. American businesses like Starbucks, McDonald's, Hardee's, Baskin Robbins, and Safeway lined the streets alongside restaurants like Roma, Korean Palace, and Taste of Shanghai.

But the biggest surprise was yet to come. For I would soon discover that a generation of Saudi women, educated in the West, holding American Ph.D.s, had returned home to revolutionize women's education in the kingdom.

Women were first allowed to enroll in universities in 1960, but they were not allowed to actually attend any classes, remembers Dr. Hend Majid Al-Khuthaila, a full professor at King Saud University and well-known writer. Instead, they were all independent studies students. They were given the books and the materials and they took the exams at the end of the semester.

In 1961, women were allowed to matriculate, attending classes in rented buildings and watching the male professors lecture via closed-circuit television.

Rather than receive what her father considered a substandard education at home, Dr. Hend was sent by her family to the United States to study in the 1970s and received her Ph.D. in higher education administration from Syracuse University in New York. When she returned to Saudi Arabia, she became the first female dean of a university in 1984. She was put in charge of the Women's College Center at King Saud University, which is the kingdom's most selective school. Although women could study for a Ph.D. degree at the university, conditions were still rather poor.

"At the time, we were housed in a few rented buildings and we had only 2,800 female students," Dr. Hend recalls. She fought to change that and succeeded. "When I left the deanship in 1992, we had twenty-five buildings which the university owned and 17,000 female students!"

Dr. Hend, an energetic woman in her mid-forties, has since become something of a celebrity in her own country. She still teaches at the university, has published five books on education, writes a weekly newspaper column on social and education issues, and has been interviewed by Liz Cheney (the vice president's daughter and a deputy assistant secretary at the U.S. Department of State) as well as Barbara Walters. She was recently named one of the three Most Influential Women in the Middle East by the Heya media organization. She herself founded two charity organizations.

She remembers that at the time when she was first sent to study in the United States in 1971, it was considered imprudent to send a daughter there alone. Her father's family actually tried to prevent her from going, arriving at the airport on the day of her departure—armed and ready to bodily remove her from the plane if necessary. Her father argued with them on the tarmac, and eventually the extended family relented, and off she went to America.

Now all three of her daughters have studied in the U.S. and her son is preparing to leave this fall for America. In fact, her oldest daughter recently returned from Boston with a master's degree in law and became the first Saudi woman to open her own law firm, called Dar Samah for Legal Consultations, specifically aimed at female clients.

Dr. Hend is proud of the progress Saudi women have made, but she is dismayed that their image in the West remains mired in stereotypes of the past.

"They think we are 'oppressed' by our culture! It's not true. We can do anything!" she insists. "It just takes someone to be the first to do something to prove it."

Administrators at the new Prince Sultan Private College for Women agree. It is the first private college for women and opened only three years ago.

"We have a very advanced curriculum," says Dr. Fadia Saud Alsaleh, dean of the college. "All our students are required to take computer courses and not only are the textbooks in English, but the language of instruction is also entirely in English." Students are also required to take math and physical education in addition to courses for their major.

The college currently offers three majors—applied linguistics, translation, and computational linguistics—but plans to expand quickly, offering various business majors and even a program in interior design in the next year or two.

Dr. Fadia received her Ph.D. in English Literature from the University of Washington in Seattle. She has put her background to good use, she says, developing a special Preparatory Year Program in intensive English to help students straight out of high school improve their language skills so that they can handle the college's advanced curriculum.

She says many aspects of her American education and experiences inform her work. "We are very interested in learning foreign culture and foreign literature, exposing ourselves to different ways of thinking and living. We can use certain things and not use other things which contradict our culture and traditions."

Like many American liberal art colleges, the school boasts of small 15:1 student-teacher ratios (unheard of in the large, crowded public Saudi universities), state-of-the-art technology-wired classrooms, and one computer per student. Also, unlike Saudi public universities, which are free, the college charges an American-style tuition.

The chair of the school's computer science department is also a graduate of an American university. Dr. Hana Al-Modaimeegh received her B.A. from King Saud University in Riyadh and her Ph.D. from George Washington University in Washington, D.C, where she also worked as a research assistant.

Her years in the United States helped convince her of the importance of learning about technology. "If you don't know how to use computers in the future, it's almost going to be like not knowing how to read or write."

One aspect of American life that occasionally distressed Dr. Hana was the stereotypes about Saudi women, particularly that women could not have careers but were housebound because of the culture's emphasis on the family. Or worse, Saudi women were perceived as rich princesses interested only in shopping.

"There is a problem of unemployment," she concedes, "but when someone has technology skills with good qualifications, it's extremely rare. Whether a man or a woman, you'll definitely find a good position."

Because Saudi society remains segregated by sex, work opportunities for women currently are available mostly in special banks for women, education, and businesses that cater to women. Women at this point in time cannot study to become engineers. The one field where men and women can work side by side, however, is medicine.

When I visit a Saudi hospital, I am surprised to find male and female doctors in the same wards, serving the same patients. The women wear headscarves but the same white lab coats as their male counterparts.

When I ask how hospitals have come to be integrated, the doctors shrug. "All hospitals here have always been like this," explains Dr. Sulaiman Assuhaimi, medical director of Security Forces Hospital. He then points out that Saudi medical colleges graduate equal numbers of male and female students and that doctors can see patients of either sex. "Even urology," he adds.

Male and female doctors receive the same salaries and all the women I spoke with insisted that they felt they had equal opportunities for promotion. In fact, they pointed out that the heads of the ophthalmology division and the OB/GYN division at the hospital were women.

The hospital also boasts the first female to become an administrator, Taghreed Samman, who is currently director of Health Education. Taghreed was educated in America, receiving her B.A. in social services and psychology at Chapman University in California and her M.A. in Public Administration from the University of Southern California in the early 1980s.

Because of Taghreed's unique position, she is a frequent commentator on Saudi television, appearing on such shows as *Good Morning Saudi,* to talk about health and social issues. Articulate and well-versed in cross-cultural differences, she can quickly tick off all the achievements Saudi women have obtained in the last couple decades. "Did you know the first uterine transplant in the world was conducted by a female Saudi surgeon [in 2000 by Dr. Wafa Mohammed Fageeh]?" she asks happily.

But she is also aware of the stereotypes.

"When I first went to America, people asked me, "Do you have a tent? Do you have an oil field in your backyard? Do you have a camel?" she laughs. "I love America, I lived there many years, and I also love my own country. I think people have the wrong impression of us because they remember that one movie [*Lawrence of Arabia*] and they don't realize how much we've changed." She sighs. "It's true that we can't drive here. But that doesn't mean we can't get around. We all have drivers. Or we can take a taxi. Or a male member of our family can take us where we need to go. All of our workplaces provide transportation if a woman doesn't have her own car. We're not stranded at home."

In fact, the only person I encountered who was openly critical of Saudi Arabia's policy against women driving was a Saudi man, who had received his M.A. from Georgetown and now worked in the government. "It's ridiculous that women can't drive here!" he exclaimed to me privately. "It's as though we are looking at our two hands and pretending one is crippled even though it is perfectly fine. It makes no sense. And economically how much do you think it costs the government to pay for all these drivers for women so that they can go to work? And what about poor women? Women without male relatives? How will they ever afford to take a taxi to even look for a job!"

Taghreed concedes that to outsiders Saudi Arabia can be difficult to understand, especially in the way it clings to traditions.

"But you know, things are changing," she says. "Already in Dubai [the capital of the neighboring United Arab Emirates], women can drive. They are working in the government. Someday it may change here, too. But when we're ready for it."

For their part, the students I encountered were not worried about Western stereotypes about Saudi women nor about their own ability to make their mark on the world.

"I guess television has given Americans this concept that we are oppressed. You don't see an *abaya* [the traditional black gown Saudi women wear in public]. You see a woman who is a slave," says Prince Sultan College first-year student Dana Al-Mandil, rolling her eyes.

No woman wears her abaya indoors in her own home or at work if she works in an all-female environment. In fact all the women I interviewed at university campuses were dressed fashionably—Dr. Fadia in a celadon-colored suit and Dr. Hana in a yellow chiffon blouse with matching skirt, for example—because no men are allowed on campus. Every Saudi woman must slip the black robe on over her clothes, however, before going out into public. She also covers her hair with a black scarf. (As a foreign woman, I was required to do neither, but long-term residents from the West could be seen walking through the streets of Riyadh, wearing abayas but not head coverings.)

Although the Koran requires Muslim women to cover themselves so that only their faces and hands are visible to men who are not family members, the color black is not actually specified in the holy book but in fact dates from Saudi traditional clothing.

"Let me tell you something about the abaya," Dana, 20, continues. "I feel very comfortable in it. It's very easy to wear. I don't have to worry about makeup or what I'm wearing. I can just put it on and go anywhere. And besides they're very fashionable!" Dana notes that it's possible to buy abaya with lacework on the sleeves, shiny beadwork, colorful embroidery, even denim cuffs. "My friends in America, they all want me to send them a jeans abaya, and they're not even Muslim!" she laughs.

What most worries the women I interviewed are media images that conflate all Saudis with terrorists. They note it has been increasingly difficult for students to obtain visas to study in the United States. As U.S. college graduates, many of the administrators I spoke with are afraid that both countries will suffer if the cultural exchange is cut off or severely restricted.

"As human beings," Dr. Hana says, "we [Americans and Saudis] share the same goals." Others were more blunt.

"Fifteen Saudis were involved in September 11 and now the whole region is going to have to pay for it?" Dr. Hend exclaims. "The media says I don't like America? How can I not like America? At one point, 15,000 Saudis were going to school in America and now they say we don't like America?" She throws up her hands in exasperation.

"I always wanted to visit the United States," sighs Dr. Shadia H. Sheikh, vice dean of the Women's Center for University Studies at King Saud University. She herself was educated at Leeds College in England. "But now, no. I'm afraid to go. Maybe they won't like me there." The current assistant dean of the College of Higher Education at King Saud, Dr. Ebtisam A. M. Sadiq, concurs. Although Dr. Ebtisam received her Ph.D. in English Literature from Wayne State University in Detroit and still loves to read American literature, including the works of John Updike, Toni Morrison, and her former advisor, Charles Baxter, she, too, now feels afraid to travel to the United States.

The nephew of a close family friend has been imprisoned for a year after a traffic accident, she says, because he had the same name as someone on a terrorist list. "I know this family personally! They're good people! It's impossible—he's not a terrorist!" she exclaims, almost in tears.

"It's really horrifying, the turn the relationship [between the U.S. and Saudi Arabia] has taken." Dr. Ebtisam shakes her head. "It hurts."

(Author's note: I have used the common Saudi practice of referring to people by their title and first names rather than by their family names. This essay was written for this volume.)

CHAPTER 19
Banks for Women

Douglas Martin

In the male-dominated society of Saudi Arabia, religion, government, business, finance, and the media are the almost exclusive preserves of men. In tradition and still largely in fact, women are expected to hide behind a black veil and stay at home to rear the children who represent the future of this thinly populated kingdom.

Despite their inferior social status, however, Saudi women have plenty of money—an estimated 30 to 40 percent of the hundreds of billions of dollars of private wealth in this country—and the Koran guarantees them personal control over it.

As a result, banks run by women and catering solely to women have begun to spring up in the major cities of Saudi Arabia. This is an unusual development in a country governed by strict interpretations of Islamic fundamentalism.

"God gave us the right to use our own money freely," Madawi al-Hassoun, director of the women's branch of the Al Rajhi Company for Trade and Commerce, said over tea in her institution's tastefully decorated lobby, "We used to feel out of place in banks."

Before women's banks began opening two years ago, many Saudi women either did not use banks or asked a family member or chauffeur to do their banking for them. Now there are four women's banks in this Red Sea port city and nine elsewhere in Saudi Arabia.

"The minute they were opened, women decided to transfer their accounts to the women's branches," said Muneira Abdellatif, manager of the women's branch of the National Commercial Bank. "Women here are more comfortable dealing with women."

The new banks for women are part of a larger struggle in Saudi society. The eventual outcome is considered crucial to Middle Eastern stability as well as to the world's energy needs. It is a battle that pits liberals against conservatives.

The liberals argue that women must be brought into the labor force to reduce the vast number of foreign workers who have flooded Saudi Arabia. The conservatives, some of whom oppose the women's banks, caution against drifting away from proven ways.

A New Kind of Progress

Women often feel caught in the middle. "All my friends talk about change, but we can't change," a university student complained.

The women's banks represent a kind of progress that many Saudis say would have been impossible as recently as five years ago. At the Al Rajhi branch, for example, women drop their veils and abas to discuss the intricacies of financial deals with trained advisers who also are women.

"The girls are very interested in gold," said Mrs. Hassoun, who was wearing large gold and diamond earrings, a gold belt, an enormous diamond ring, and a gold hairpiece. In addition, her eyelids were sprinkled with gold sequins.

Mrs. Hassound said her customers had purchased some 50,000 ounces of gold—worth about $18.5 million at present prices—at the bank and stored it there. Neither she nor other women bankers, however, would say how many customers they have or how much money their deposits add up to.

Women's banks, such as the one run by the National Commercial Bank, offer the same range of banking services as the men's banks do: checking, letters of credit, personal loans, business loans, traveler's checks, safety deposit boxes, and stockbroker service for trading in Saudi companies' shares.

Ambiguous View of Saving

Saving accounts are less clear-cut. Under Islamic law, making a profit from interest is regarded as sinful. Modern customers are given the choice of whether they prefer to earn five percent yield or nothing on their savings. In Saudi Arabia a five percent yield is considered quite acceptable because the cost of living here has been rising only three or four percent a year (mainly because of heavy government subsidies).

Al Rajhi, by comparison, offers somewhat fewer financial services in both its women's and men's divisions because its primary purpose is to exchange foreign currencies. Al Rajhi and a host of similar institutions, which are not regulated by the Saudi monetary authorities, date from this country's colorful trading past and remain an integral part of its financial system.

Saudi women, who for centuries have been restricted to a sheltered existence, are still not allowed to drive cars. To them, the new banks represent something of a haven away from home. The women's banks feature elegant decor and stuffed armchairs, and they serve tea and coffee. The women's branch of Al Rajhi, for instance, has royal blue and white wallpaper, a painting (done by a female artist) of a Bedouin group at sunset and a religious scene in elaborate needlepoint.

The National Commercial Bank's branch for women is furnished in a soft beige and brown, while the Saudi British Bank's branch presents subtle tones of green and gray illuminated with soft lights.

The bank's efforts to attract women customers would seem worthwhile. Although Saudi women receive only half the inheritance of men, they are granted full control over their funds by the Koran. For years, analysts say, women investors in Saudi Arabia have been putting money into sound holdings such as real estate, thereby increasing their assets.

Some women are even using capital to go into business for themselves. Although the number of women entrepreneurs remains small, they own and operate boutiques, tailoring establishments, hair styling salons, restaurants, and light manufacturing plants.

The demand for business loans to women is growing.

This economic assertiveness has been paralleled by a campaign for women to participate more fully in Saudi society. Increasingly, Saudi women are being educated, often through the university level. This movement reflects a policy adopted by the male-dominated government. By 1985 the number of classrooms for female students is expected to be 4,305, up from 210 in 1980, and the number of such students is expected to be up 47 percent, to nearly 700,000. [Editor's note: For current statistics, compare this chapter with Part Four, Chapter 29.]

"I think the real purpose of the ladies' banks is not to provide any services they did not have before in the existing banks," said a Saudi man who works as a translator for an engineering firm. "It's to give all these smart women something to do."

Mrs. Hassoun, in part, agrees. Applications for employment at her bank number between 600 and 700, she said, but none of her fourteen current employees would dream of leaving. "The applicants are not in need of money, they are in need of killing time," she said. "They want to wake up in the morning with some purpose in life." Until now, the few careers open to Saudi women have been mainly in nursing and education.

All the women's bank branches make a point of hiring Saudi women as part of the country's "Saudization" drive. The National Commercial Bank, for instance, has whittled its number of expatriate women employees—first hired because they had banking experience—from ten to four. The bank's total number of female workers remains stable at sixteen.

Sometimes the husbands of these bank employees have expressed resentment at their wives' newfound interest outside the home. But much of the male reaction has been in the form of good-natured ribbing.

"I think the men are jealous," Mrs. Abdellatif said with a laugh. "We're not dependent on them anymore."

A Start toward Equality?

Even the staunchest liberals acknowledge that the new banks are only a small step toward full equality for Saudi women. But sociological experts say the trend could be irreversible, especially with women's mushrooming educational achievement.

CHAPTER 20
Crime and Punishment

Robin Wright

Every Friday, as the megaphones echo the chanting whine that marks the midway call to prayer, a small crowd begins to gather around the square between the main mosque and the sprawling square in the Saudi capital.

They are waiting for the centuries-old tradition of weekly public punishment of criminals. But the crowds more often than not disperse after a few minutes, for there are few public punishments these days.

As the rest of the world sorts out year-end statistics and percentage increases, the Saudis will probably be among the few—if not the only—to boast of dramatic decreases in crime.

The Interior Ministry claims various types of murders and attempts were down, in the Islamic year 1401, by 20 to 35 percent. But there were few to begin with; in a country of some 8.5 million, the Saudis recorded only eighty-seven premeditated murders and twenty-one manslaughter cases, plus 160 attempts and sixty-five threats.

Theft, the biggest single offense in the kingdom, was down 28 percent. The statistics reflect the general air of security in Saudi Arabia, where a visitor feels no hesitation about momentarily stepping away from a briefcase or purse. Much like the Chinese, the Saudis have such a polite reverence for personal property that any item left behind, even thrown away, in one Saudi city often will catch up with a visitor in the next.

After theft, the biggest crime in the austere Gulf state was the consumption, possession, or manufacture of alcohol, all strictly forbidden by Islamic law. That, and unspecified "moral" crimes, were the only offenses that went up, however slightly.

The Saudis, who live by one of the strictest moral codes in the world, take their crime problem seriously, remarkably small though it is. All laws in the kingdom are based on the Koran and the teachings of the seventh-century prophet Muhammad. Justice is administered by religious courts.

The motivation of the House of Saud in unifying the country, and the basis of its legitimacy today, has been the spread of this strict religious code, known as Wahhabism.

Indeed, the most active threats to the government have come not from reformists but from religious fundamentalists, as seen during the attack on the Grand Mosque in 1979. The fundamentalists oppose introduction of "corrupting" influences such as television, women's education, and soccer.

Thus many of the ancient sentences, used in the time of Muhammad, are still employed today, as seen in the controversial film *Death of a Princess*. This is a portrayal of the sad saga of Princess Misha'al Bint Fahd Bin Muhammad, who was shot for adultery and whose lover was beheaded.

Yet Western diplomats say the Saudis have tried quietly to phase out or lower the number of what Westerners consider barbaric punishments. One such diplomat commented after two years of experience in Saudi Arabia that to his knowledge during his assignment there were only two beheadings for criminal offenses. (By contrast, after the attack on the Grand Mosque, sixty-three of the accused were beheaded in various cities throughout the kingdom for this treasonous offense.)

"It's only in extreme cases with repeat offenders that you're likely to see those kinds of sentences anymore. They're rarely imposed any more, even the whippings for morality offenses, which are still a very touchy matter here," commented a European political attaché.

Yet in what outsiders might interpret as an ironic twist, caning or corporal punishment in schools has always been banned. And the Saudi founding father, Abdul Aziz Ibn Saud, publicly forgave some of the tribal factions that fought against him. Occasionally he incorporated opposition leaders, who might normally have been killed, into his government.

Government officials claim foreign influence—there are more than one million foreign workers in the oil-rich nation—and the pressure of rapid modernization are responsible for much of today's crime in Saudi Arabia. They point out that some 34 percent of all offenses were committed by non-Saudis.

These two factors are also responsible for white-collar crime, according to the Commerce Ministry. Dishonest middlemen have moved in quickly to take advantage of the overnight wealth of many that are uneducated or unfamiliar with the standard of goods their money should buy.

The jewelry business is one of the prime targets for fraud. Some foreign exporters peddle low-quality gold as 18-karat or try to pass off rhinestones as diamonds. To combat the problem, the Saudi Arabian Standard Organization (SASO) has started surprise inspections, using disguised ministry employees, who buy five different types of jewelry in randomly selected shops. The gems are tested for authenticity.

Gold jewelry has long been an important part of Saudi culture as well as a common way of investing money because bank accounts were once discouraged by the Islamic code that prohibits making interest. Ministry officials claim the sale of jewelry in Saudi Arabia averages between $25 and $33 million a day.

To stamp out fraud, the SASO has also introduced specifications on imported goods, ranging from construction materials to milk. Commerce Undersecretary Abdul Rahman al Zamil recently said a new statute on commercial fraud was in the works, and that the government hoped eventually to eliminate a large sector of intermediaries by setting up a company to act as purchaser and supplier, beginning with agricultural products.

"Like everything else here, the level of all kinds of crime is a function of staggering growth and lack of preparedness in coping with it," remarked a Western envoy. "Without it there would probably be so little common crime as to be negligible. Hard as it may be to understand, it is just not part of their culture."

CHAPTER 21
From Bedouins to Oil Barons

William R. Polk

[Editor's note: This article is a review of three books on Saudi Arabia: *The House of Saud* by David Holden and Richard Johns; *The Kingdom* by Robert Lacy; and *Saudi Arabia in the 1980s* by William B. Quandt.]

Until a few years ago, few in the West thought of Arabia as more than a sand lot suitable for a Rudolph Valentino movie or the site visited by Muslim pilgrims. Unlike most of the surrounding countries, Arabia had never been conquered or colonized by Western powers—its poverty was a far better defense than rivers or mountains—and its religious commitment made it impervious to the missionaries so active elsewhere in Africa and the Middle East. The population was small and scattered, and few of its children had the means or the interest to go abroad to study.

Even when oil was struck, just before World War II, the initial impact was small. The fields were distant from the major population centers and the pipeline was along a remote frontier. Because little local processing was done, relatively few Saudis even knew that they had oil. And, in those days oil was not worth very much. For a generation it remained cheap. In 1950, before Saudi production amounted to much, oil was only $2 a barrel. Twenty years later, measured in 1950 dollars, the price had fallen to about $1.79 a barrel. In 1970, the total revenue of Saudi Arabia was far less than a middle-sized American city.

Then the changes began. Saudi Arabia embarked upon a major development program and the price of oil soared. Today, the country earns in three days what it earned in all of 1970.

Take some comparisons: thirty years ago, Saudis thought of their central bank as a strong room for the storage of gold coins—the room did not have to be very large. Today its Monetary Agency (SAMA) controls investments of about $100 billion throughout the industrial world and is the biggest purchaser of U.S. Treasury notes. In 1950, the country had almost no roads, which meant that travel to many regions amounted to expeditions; today superhighways criss-cross the country. Then its few telephones were virtually inoperative even across town in the capital; today one can dial direct from even the most remote sites to any other "modern" center in the world more easily than in most of Europe and much of America. Then there was virtually no public entertainment and little education other than rudimentary religious schools; today, television reaches into every house and virtually every family has dozens, many have thousands, of videotapes from Japan, Europe, and America, while free education—up to and including the universities of Europe and America—is the citizen's right. In 1950 even minor ailments required treatment abroad but today huge medical complexes tower over all the cities.

In the avalanche of the new, much of the old has simply vanished. The desert today is truly deserted because the Bedouin have sought the cities' bright lights. Walled villages have been submerged beneath concrete, glass, and asphalt. Documenting the passing of the old is easier than discerning the pattern of the new. The Saudis have had little time for nostalgia; for them the past often means pain, privation, and weakness. But in the rush toward the new, of course, must also be elements of the traditional way of life. And it is there, in national identity, religion, family, and wealth, rather than in the dramatic commercial or economic statistics, that the incomprehensibility of Saudi Arabia arises.

All this would be merely interesting or at least quaint, however crucial for the Saudis, but for the fact that Saudi Arabia is the major source for the petroleum that fires Western and Japanese industry and provides the raw material for the petrochemical industry upon which we increasingly rely for our daily necessities. As Robert Lacey put it tartly, "If it was not for a freak of geology, few people in the Western world would give a fig about King Khalid and his falcons." But they must, because not only do the Saudi fields contain about a quarter of the world's oil but they are expected to last long after those of most other countries, including the United States and the Soviet Union, are well drained. Even today, with the "loss" of Iran and the hostility of Libya, Saudi Arabian oil has become of prime importance to America and shortly will become attractive to the Soviet Union.

America, too, has changed over the past generation and no longer can afford to think of the world just as pieces of a strategic puzzle or solely in terms of our own interests. Now we realize that we must try to find out what the world looks like from the other side. That is the issue set for us by these three books reviewed in this chapter. Their approaches are different and each has something unique to offer the reader.

In their book, *The House of Saud,* authors David Holden and Richard Johns present a detailed history of the ruling family of Arabia. David Holden was, until his mysterious murder in Cairo four years ago, the chief correspondent for the *London Sunday Times* and widely regarded as one of the best journalists operating in the Middle East. His unfinished task was taken up by Richard Johns of the *London Financial Times* who, while lacking Holden's long exposure to the Middle East, has made the more modern issues of oil and money his special concern. The division of tasks and styles shows in the book and leaves it, while full of fascinating detail, without clear focus. Of the three, however, it is the one anyone visiting Arabia would find most useful; of the three, it is perhaps the most pessimistic on the future of the regime.

Robert Lacey's book, *The Kingdom*, is more interestingly written. Less a history than *The House of Saud*, it has some of the virtues of a small-town newspaper, full of gossip that makes its characters seem, if not exactly like the folks down the street, at least recognizably human. But more attractive I suspect for those who chose it as a Book-of-the-Month Club offering and who have engaged Lacey as a new guru on Arabia is his ability to put into a paragraph or two the essence of fairly complex issues like the source of wealth of the Saudi royal princess, the change of oil prices, the issue of corruption in Arabia, and the Palestine issue as the Arabs see it. For example, and showing some of his failures and mistakes, Lacey finds in him [Faisal] elements of greatness. His discussion of Saud, the black sheep king, is especially humane and insightful in crediting the fallen king for his role in beginning educational and welfare programs while at the same time documenting his incompetence and wastefulness. These portraits, "warts and all," are not in the Arab tradition, and Lacey mentions, almost casually, that his book is banned in Arabia "on the basis of eighty-two objections," but in it, the Saudis emerge more understandable and more likable than they have appeared before even in books they commissioned.

William Quandt, who served as a Middle Eastern specialist on the National Security Council during the Carter Administration, undertakes a very different sort of task in his book *Saudi Arabia in the 1980s*. In effect, he tries to think through the issues facing Saudi Arabia today as though he were planning Saudi policy. He has written the sort of work many diplomats wish a Saudi had written; Saudi unwillingness or inability to articulate or analyze major issues in ways similar to those we employ, or try to employ, in foreign policy planning has been one of the most confusing aspects of the Arab-American dialogue. King Faisal, for example, often reduced world problems to the twin—for him even identical—threats of Zionism and Communism. And Quandt, imagining a Riyadh perspective, shows the complexity of the world the Saudis face. Yet it is the Palestine issue with which Quandt (and the real Saudis) begin: "As long as the Palestinian issue festers, the Saudis fear, the surrounding Arab world will be threatened by instability, the Soviets will be a source of arms and diplomatic support for some Arab regimes, and Saudi Arabia will be asked to use its oil to force the Americans to extract concessions from the Israelis." Religion also is involved deeply. The moral justification for the Saudi regime arises from its origins in and commitment to the preservation of Islam, and failure in this area could cause the overthrow of the regime in the future if the sentiments that caused the November 1979 Mecca incident become better focused. Rivalry with Egypt also is an ingredient, as is genuine concern about Israeli occupation of Saudi territory and simulated attacks on a Saudi air base.

Saudi Arabia, riding its wave of oil-generated riches, faces new realities. It can no longer take refuge in its poverty, but along with greater opportunities must cope with new dangers. Its relationship with the United States is changing and must change. Its newly educated younger people will no longer allow it to do otherwise, and recognition of the American special relationship with Israel, never understood by the Saudis, becomes the occasion for ever more heated and frequent disagreements. Quandt notes that already, "Little remains of the confidence and goodwill that characterized the relationship in some earlier periods." And, partly as a consequence of this, there is a discernible shift in the relationship with the Soviet Union.

In what Quandt calls "Operation Charm," beginning in January 1979, the Russians began to make gestures toward the kingdom. By July 1980, Saudi Foreign Minister Saud Fisal could state that if the Russians withdrew from Afghanistan, all inhibitions to good relations between the two countries would be removed. As the Soviet need for imported oil grows in the 1980s, this tendency to find a workable relationship will undoubtedly accelerate. Then, sophisticated Soviet use of the stick of pressure from the radical Arab regimes over the Palestine issue and the carrot of massive arms supply will be formidable indeed.[1]

Will Saudi Arabia survive?

As mentioned, Johns is pessimistic. He ends *The House of Saud* with a comment by an earlier observer of the old Arabia on the ruins of the first Saudi capital outside Riyadh. The words, he says, rang true to him in 1981:

> Wahhabism was in ruin. The capital, bigger, wealthier and richer in palaces than any town in Central Arabia had ever been before, was witness of a ruin that was greater, immeasurably greater, than that first ruin because this time the ruin was spiritual.

> "But the Kingdom is still in being," writes Johns.

Quandt is less impressionistic but also less clear. Having noted all the predictable danger points, particularly the growth of the modern armed forces that have given rise to the other Middle Eastern coups, he says that "one should resist the temptation to try to predict how long the Saudi regime will remain in power. Suffice it to say that the regime will be obliged to change, to adapt, and to improvise if it is to continue." That is both to state the obvious and to back away from what every government and business remotely connected with Arabia must undertake. Because the answer to the question could so deeply affect all of our lives, the "temptation" will be felt by us all.

Finally, Lacey gives what might be regarded as a Saudi answer: the world and wealth are transitory. All comes from and returns to God. And in daily experience, the desert, even with its privation and poverty, offers a solace difficult for those who have not known it to appreciate.

> This is where they have come from. The desert is the source of everything they hold dear—their religion, their code of honor, their ancestry, their black gold—and regularly the inhabitants of the Kingdom flee the modern pyramids their riches are creating to the bleak void that they find so consoling. There, the Saudis like to say, their ancestors returned after having conquered half the known world in the 7th century, and to the desert they could again return if this great oily bubble of theirs explodes.

ENDNOTE

1. Editor's note: As the reader can see from this article, it was all but impossible in the 1980s for Saudi specialists to imagine the changes the world would undergo over the next twenty years. Today of course the Soviet Union no longer exists—Russia is struggling with its own inability to resolve its difficulties with the Islamic-dominated republic of Chechnya and must deal with radical Islamic terrorism on its own soil. The Palestinian issue—lack of statehood—remains as the most important unresolved issue that divides how Western secular nations and Middle Eastern Islamic nations view their relations. This chapter is one of the articles provided to give the reader historic perspective on the issue and also to pose the reader with the following questions: Because we have not resolved this issue and the world has changed in ways unimaginable to this author twenty years ago, how does the reader propose to resolve the Palestinian issue? What forces will provide pressure on radical Islamic groups today? Can the reader try to imagine a solution so that the world will not have to be faced with the same dilemma in another twenty years?

PART THREE
THE WAR AGAINST TERRORISM

CHAPTER 22
Saudi Arabia, on a Dagger's Edge

Faye Bowers

RIYADH, SAUDI ARABIA—They're not Felix and Oscar, although they are a somewhat odd couple. One is a bit impish. He looks like a young Omar Sharif and sports a Vandyke beard—like Robert DeNiro, his favorite movie star.

The other looks more scholarly. He wears wire-rimmed glasses and is extremely serious. His favorite philosopher is Nietzsche.

The two, however, have similar backgrounds and goals. Khalid al-Ghannami and Mansour al-Nogaidan were once subversive sheikhs, religious leaders espousing the same tenets as Osama bin Laden and his acolytes.

But they both embarked on spiritual journeys—separately—and now embrace a more moderate, inclusive view of Islam, and act as the most outspoken public boosters of religious reform in Saudi Arabia.

In fact, they made 180-degree turns from far right to left, and now say they want a broad reformation of Islam, something akin to what they say John Calvin or Martin Luther kicked off in Christianity. That's no small quest in any part of the Muslim world, much less Saudi Arabia. As the birthplace of Islam, Saudi Arabia adheres to a branch of the religion known to many people as Wahhabism, as well as tribal cultural traditions. The struggle over how to interpret Islam politically is not only important for Saudi Arabia, but for many foreign countries that receive billions of dollars in aid from Saudi Arabia—for building mosques, supplying copies of the Koran, and teaching their brand of Islam.

Wahhabism has led many Muslims to support and even join jihadist groups from Asia to Europe and the U.S., according to several government officials. And changing the ideology that supports and advocates the use of violence is crucial to eliminating terror attacks, like those perpetrated by Al Qaeda.

Change Wrought with Bombs

That these two sheikhs are now free—to a certain extent—to speak out, is testament to changes thanks in no small part to the May and November suicide bombings in Saudi Arabia.

Since those attacks, particularly the November 8 attack that targeted the Muhaya compound where mostly Arabs lived—and died—the Saudi government has acknowledged that it has a problem with religious extremists.

It has created a public dialogue on these thorny issues within society and has vowed to reform or remove those clerics who promote extremism or advocate the use of violence.

"A dialogue between scholars has been going on for a long time . . . but now it has become an open thing," says Abdulrahman ai-Matrodi, deputy minister for Islamic Affairs. "We have people who have been in the West. And they got more information, and maybe [have] more open minds than others who have not left. But you will not find them working against their country or their religion. They would like their religion [so] that they can follow the religion and still be modern."

This is no small task, of course, in a country that has at least 50,000 mosques and as many clerics. Not to mention the *muttawaeen,* feared religious police.

Moreover, the ruling family and conservative religious leaders have closely collaborated since the founding of this country.

At extremely opportune times, the *ulema* (religious leaders) issue *fatwas* (edicts) that enforce the princes' proclamations. For example, when, religious zealots took over the Grand Mosque in Mecca at the end of the 1979 hajj (religious pilgrimage), the religious establishment issued a fatwa that allowed government troops to retake the mosque.

Now the government has to find a stable middle ground between the extremists, following in the footsteps of Osama bin Laden; the arch-conservative Muslims, who make up the religious establishment; and those who want to be far more open, like Mr. Ghannami and Mr. Nogaidan.

One European diplomat based in Riyadh says that the struggle is now between the government and the fundamentalist sheikhs. "The government has made some important gains," he says. But it has a long way to go, and it won't be easy.

Khalil al-Khalil, a professor of political science at Imam Muhammed bin Saud Islamic University in Riyadh, concurs. He even goes further, as do several other educators and intellectuals, saying it will be difficult for the government to make changes with some stalwart leaders of the religious community. In particular, he says, that the Ministry of Islamic Affairs is not cooperative and the minister needs to be replaced.

"The minister of Islamic Affairs is very behind, and the man is not really cooperating," Khalil says. "He is probably there by mistake." But, he goes on to say, the royal family has the power to enforce change—especially because it controls the purse strings.

"The clerics are employed by the government, and if the government decides something, the clerics have to listen," says al-Khalil, who also is a member of the government's commission on education reform. "They are cooperating so far."

The government has, for example, removed some 2,000 clerics for violating "prohibitions against the preaching of intolerance," and has sent back 1,500 for additional training in more moderate interpretations of Koranic verses and current events. It has begun a program to tamp down the zealousness of the mutawaeen. And it has arrested three clerics for issuing fatwas promoting terrorist activity. All have since gone on television to recant their views.

Ghannami and Nogaidan, however, are skeptical about such conversions. They doubt these clerics changed their views so completely in only a few months.

For them, the journey from extremism to tolerance was a long one—at least five years, they say. Ghannami, now a middle school English teacher, was introduced in the late 1990s to more moderate Egyptian and Moroccan clerics by a friend. He used to sneak to the friend's house to watch them on television, and he read hundreds of their books, which preached love of life, human values, and tolerance.

Nogaidan spent a considerable period of time in jail for extremist activities, like burning down video stores in 1992 because he viewed them as heretical to Islam. While in jail, he was introduced to a moderate Palestinian cleric, several treatises on the history of the West, and the works of prominent Western philosophers.

Both gradually began to question quietly at first, and then openly, the interpretation of Islam they and thousands like them—many of whom are now dedicated to Al Qaeda or other terrorist groups—received in Saudi Arabia's schools and mosques.

"Religious leaders say music is forbidden, photographs are forbidden, MTV is forbidden, sex lives are forbidden," says Ghannammi. "These young men who blow themselves up in Saudi Arabia, it's because of the teaching in the mosques and the schools. [It] concentrates on the life after this life. This life to them is just a gas station, someplace to stop and refill and move on to something better for eternity."

Ghannami, who also writes occasional newspaper columns, goes on to say that many of the extremists also practice *takfir*. That means if one Muslim deems another Muslim a *takfir* (an infidel), a fatwa can be issued targeting that infidel.

He goes on to say that the difference between him, Nogaidan, and others who were schooled in the same way and Osama bin Laden and other Al Qaeda members is that the latter went to Afghanistan and trained in a "military way."

Ghannami and Nodaidan—as well as many others in this country—point out that it was the U.S. collaborating with Saudi Arabia in sending and funding the *mujahideen* operations in Afghanistan in the 1980s.

Both men also have suffered because of their now-public conversions. Nodaidan, who is a regular columnist for *Al Riyadh* newspaper in Riyadh, was targeted because of his views with a fatwa by one of the sheiks now jailed.

He also was picked up by the religious police in November and sentenced to seventy-five lashes for his columns criticizing Wahhabism. The sentence was later suspended. But the two say they walk a fine line between criticism of the religious establishment and advocating reform.

Many of their former friends—who are still extremists—have "forsaken" them, and they say they receive hundreds of threatening letters and phone calls.

Others say the number of these extremist *imams* is small and does not represent the mainstream.

"These imams are few, and don't have the support of big, well-known sheikhs and imams," says Nasser al-Rasheed, a conservative Saudi businessman who was educated in the U.S. "Their attitudes are not created because of the Wahhabi belief, but because they went to fight in Afghanistan and because of the U.S. position regarding Israel."

A force to be feared?

Sheikh Mussa al-Hanagid concurs. He is a member of the muttawaeen. The muttawaeen have long been caricatured—and feared. They are depicted as elderly men with long white beards, robes, and sticks—mainly screaming at women to cover more fully.

Sheikh Mussa says the government is recalibrating the roles of religious police, too. Mussa, himself a trainer, says there are a number of supervisors monitoring the muttawaeen. They are being trained to be more tolerant, kind, and professional. For example, they've now all been ordered to wear badges with pictures that clearly identify them.

Ghannami and Nogaidan are skeptical of the changes and think the government needs to go further. "We must find a new reading of our religion that is more tolerant, something that will fit better with globalization and communicating with our fellow man," Ghannami says. "[Saudi Arabia] is not an isolated desert island anymore."

CHAPTER 23
How an Al Qaeda Hotbed Turned Inhospitable

Faye Bowers

RIYADH, SAUDI ARABIA—The faces are everywhere: on display in restaurants, shop windows, and the opening pages of the main daily newspapers.

They are the twenty-six most wanted young men in Saudi Arabia, sought in connection with the May 12 and November 8 suicide bombings here that took the lives of fifty-three people, mainly Arabs. But nine Americans also perished in the attacks.

The bounty on these men is high: one million Saudi riyals ($267,000) each. Supply leads on a terror cell, and you receive $1,867,000. Help foil a terrorist attack, and it's worth $1,333,000.

The rewards, along with the public display of the suspects, are part of an unprecedented campaign by the Saudi royal family to enlist everyday Saudis in this battle against Al Qaeda.

Not that long ago, after the 1996 bombing of the Khobar Towers, in which nineteen U.S. servicemen died, Saudi Arabia was an unwilling partner. It wasn't much more compliant after the September 11, 2001, attacks.

But now, with the terror group's wrath striking the royal family's home turf, the small inner circle of princes has united and is going public, reaching out to its own population and to the U.S. "This is a wholesale change for the Saudis, with the publication of these names and pictures," says a Western diplomat posted in Riyadh. "Saudi hearts and minds are what is important now."

Al Qaeda made a huge mistake by attacking Saudi Arabia, home to Islam's two holiest shrines, says Mohammed Al-Hulwah, head of the foreign relations committee of the king's Majlis Ash Shura (consultative council). "Now, the government has declared a holy war on these terrorists," he says, pumping his fists for emphasis in his typically Saudi living room. The walls, drapes, and furniture are covered in pastels with geometric designs to comply with a religious ban on portrayals of people or animals. "Some people before were sympathetic with them, but now they are really starting to think and question."

Up until this point, say Saudi and U.S. government officials, ordinary Saudis—as well as some members of the royal family—were in denial. They could not accept that fifteen of the nineteen hijackers came from this country. But with the two bombings in Saudi Arabia, ordinary Saudis have not only come to accept they have a problem with extremists, but are actively helping their government root them out.

One Saudi man, for example, phones the new government hotline recently to report that Othman al-Amri, number eleven on the most-wanted list, had stopped at his home while driving through the area. About a week earlier, someone tipped off the authorities to the location of Ibrahim al-Rayes, who was later killed by security forces. From May through the end of 2003, some 300 other terror suspects have been detained or killed, according to officials.

The Saudis also have become much more cooperative with the U.S. teams of Treasury, FBI, and CIA officers now based here, working hand in hand with Saudi officials at the Mahabith, Saudi Arabia's counterpart to the FBI. "We have very good cooperation right now," says a Western law enforcement officer based here.

These teams are beginning to establish certain patterns. For example, they've been able to trace many of the guns they've captured to both Yemen and Afghanistan. Moreover, with each arrest that is made, the teams gather additional information that leads them to others. "Every time you catch someone, they have something with them that allows [the suspect] to get to the next person [within the terror cell structure]," the law enforcement official says.

The information developed by the teams has led the Saudis to install heat-sensitive cameras and barbed-wire fences at or near the most frequently used smuggling routes along its border with Yemen. That has already begun to pay off. On December 27, Saudi officials announced they'd arrested a little more than 4,000 "infiltrators" trying to cross that border and seized a large cache of ammunition.

The cooperation includes the pursuit of financial backing for terrorists, too. Since this past spring [2003], the Saudis have instituted a number of measures to block funding: Collection boxes were removed from mosques, and tighter restrictions were placed on financial transfers and charitable donations.

But preventing personal donations to Arabs perceived to be in need—for example, Palestinians—will be much more difficult for the Saudi government to control; nearly everyone here bemoans the treatment of Palestinians by Israel.

"We have to support our brothers in Palestine," says Nasser al-Rasheed, a bespectacled conservative Mullim who has the traditional untrimmed white beard. "I would give more to a Palestinian I trust. But I would not give to Hamas [the Palestinian resistance movement placed on the U.S. list of terror organizations]. But how do you know [the difference]?"

On the international front, however, the cooperation has paid off. Last month, the

U.S. and Saudi Arabia jointly designated two European organizations as financial backers of terrorists: Bosnia-based Vazir (formerly FZ Taqwa, closed in August 2002).

Still, no one thinks the crackdown will end anytime soon. Officials estimate that between 2,000 and 10,000 *mujahideen* returned here from fighting wars in Afghanistan. "A subculture exists here, those who fell into what the Saudis refer to as *jihadist or takfiri* terminology," says the Western diplomat. "It's a group of people—60, 600, 6,000, 60,000. We don't know the exact number, but it's not infinite."

These terrorists have recently switched tactics as well, beginning to target the country's intelligence officials. On December 29, Lt. Col. Ibrahim al-Dhaleh parked his Lexus [2003] and stepped away just before it exploded. Earlier in the month, Maj. Gen. Abdelaziz al-Huweirini, number three in the intelligence service, was shot and wounded in Riyadh.

"We've got to recognize that we're fighting an ideology that springs out of a radical or xenophobic Islam," the Western diplomat says. "If we caught Osama bin Laden tomorrow, I am convinced Al Qaeda would be finished. But that won't end the war on terror. The ideology is entrenched in the Muslim world . . . We will probably be battling this for the next generation."

CHAPTER 24
No Saudi Payment to Al Qaeda is Found[1]

Douglas Jehl

WASHINGTON, JUNE 18—The staff of the September 11 commission has put forward what amounts to a major revision of a widely held perception in Washington that top Saudi officials gave money to Al Qaeda.

The new account, based on nineteen months of staff work, asserts flatly that there is "no evidence" that the Saudi government or senior Saudi officials financed the group, which is led by Osama bin Laden. In 2002, a joint Congressional committee was reported to have concluded the opposite in a classified study that was then the most extensive on the issue.

Senator Bob Graham, a Florida Democrat and cochairman of the committee that issued the report, said at the time, "In my judgment there is compelling evidence that a foreign government provided direct support through officials and agents of that government to some of the September 11 hijackers."

Although he did not name the Saudi government, those familiar with the committee's report at the time said it focused on Saudi Arabia.

The intensity of feelings in Washington about Saudi Arabia and the difficulty in tracking the flow of money mean that the issue will almost certainly remain contentious. At a minimum, the emphatic tone of the staff report and the extent of work on which it was apparently based pose a major challenge to the view that Saudi Arabia and its royal family somehow financed the September 11 attacks.

In the new report, the presidential commission on September 11 did acknowledge that Al Qaeda had "found fertile fund-raising ground" in Saudi Arabia, where "extreme religious views are common, and charitable giving is essential to the culture and until recently, subjected to very limited oversight."

Still it said, "There is no convincing evidence that any government financially supported al Qaeda before 9/11." It added, "Saudi Arabia has long been considered the primary source of Al Qaeda funding, but we found no evidence that the Saudi government as an institution or senior officials within the Saudi government funded Al Qaeda."

The effort to dispel the idea that the Saudi government played a role in supporting Al Qaeda occurred seventeen months after the Congressional committee finished its work on a report that many contended reached a very different conclusion.

The latest report is based on a broader range of interviews and much greater access to classified documents than the Congressional report, people with knowledge of both operations said.

In addition, members of the presidential commission traveled to Saudi Arabia twice in the inquiry, officials from Saudi Arabia and from the commission said.

Adel al-Jubeir, a senior adviser to Crown Prince Abdullah of Saudi Arabia, said the September 11 commission's findings "vindicate what we have been saying all along—that Saudi officials, the Saudi government, the royal family, had no role in funding whatsoever."

"One by one, the myths are being dispelled," he said.

At the time of the congressional report, the Saudi government asked that the report be made public. People who had read the report said it described senior Saudi officials as having funneled hundreds of millions of dollars to charitable groups and operatives who may have helped finance the attacks.

The revised account was detailed in a staff report that also sought to correct what it described as other widespread misperceptions involving Al Qaeda. It said that contrary to many accounts, Mr. bin Laden, who comes from a wealthy Saudi family, never inherited vast sums of money, instead, he obtained the $30 million a year needed to sustain Al Qaeda from financial facilitators who "raised money from witting and unwitting donors, primarily in the Gulf countries, and particularly in Saudi Arabia."

The section of the report by the joint congressional inquiry that addressed the role of Saudi Arabia was deleted from a nearly 900-page report that was made public last July, more than seven months after the panel finished the classified report.

The chapter focused on the role foreign governments played in the hijackings, but concentrates almost entirely on Saudi Arabia, people who have seen the section said.

The new staff report by the commission also asserts that a 1996 terrorist attack in Saudi Arabia, understood to have been carried out by a Saudi Shiite group operating with help from Iran, may also have involved support from Al Qaeda. On Friday, however, senior intelligence officials said they knew of no evidence to support such a claim.

The report said the panel had seen "strong but indirect evidence" that Mr. bin Laden's organization "did in fact, play some as yet unknown role" in the attacks on the complex, in which twenty-four people were killed, including nineteen American airmen. But United States officials have publicly stated that the attack was carried out by members of a pro-Iranian group known as Saudi Hezbollah, and the United States government has made those charges in federal court.

With highly classified documents previously inaccessible to those outside the government, the commission's staff painted a picture of Al Qaeda that differs in other important ways from what have been widespread perceptions.

It said there was "no persuasive evidence" that Al Qaeda relied on the drug trade as an important source of revenue or raised money by trafficking in diamonds in the chaotic nations of West Africa.

Mr. bin laden has less personal wealth than has been widely believed, the report says. Though he is a member of a wealthy family and received about $1 million a year until he was cut off in 1994, Mr. bin laden never received the $300 million inheritance that has become the stuff of folklore, the report said.

"Contrary to popular understanding, bin Laden did not fund Al Qaeda through a personal fortune and a network of businesses," the report said. "Instead, Al Qaeda relied primarily on a fund-raising network developed over time."

The report said that Mr. bin Laden himself was only a small contributor to Al Qaeda. But it said that the organization spent an estimated $30 million a year before the September 11 attacks, with as much as $20 million going to the Taliban government in Afghanistan, which provided Al Qaeda with a haven.

But like George J. Tenet, the director of central intelligence, and other top government officials, the [CIA] staff said it had no doubt that Al Qaeda was still "actively striving" to attack the United States, despite the blows it had suffered since September 11. The group's objective, the staff said, remains to inflict casualties even greater than the nearly 3,000 people killed on September 11, and it "remains extremely interested in conducting chemical, biological, radiological, or nuclear attacks."

"The Intelligence Community expects that the trend toward attacks intended to cause ever-higher casualties will continue," the commission said in the report titled *Overview of the Enemy*.

The report said that Mr. bin Laden had first set his sights on attacks on the United States in 1992. But it casts doubt on the idea that he and his organization played any role in the 1993 attack on the World Trade Center or the thwarted 1995 plot in Manila to blow up a dozen American airliners.

ENDNOTE

1. From the *New York Times,* June 19, 2004, reprint with permission.

CHAPTER 25
The Insurgents:
Saudis Offer Limited Amnesty to Rebels[1]

Neil MacFarquhar

JIDDA, SAUDI ARABIA, JUNE 23—The Saudi government announced a one-month amnesty on Wednesday, starting at once, for anyone involved in extremist activities. The offer suggested that the country's rulers, while shaken by two months of horrific terrorist violence, believe their grip on power to be firm.

In a speech broadcast across Saudi Arabia and the Arab world Crown Prince Abdullah vowed that those who turned themselves in over the next month would face no state prosecution although he left open the possibility for relatives of the victims to demand justice under Islamic law.

"We offer a chance for whoever belongs to the misguided group and is still at large following involvement in terrorism operations to repent, plead guilty, and voluntarily surrender," said the Crown Prince, the country's actual ruler, according to the translation provided by the Saudi Press Agency.

"We, government and people, want to open the door of penance and security for whoever is wise enough to take it; and whoever takes the chance will be safe," he added. "But should he be obstinate, he will face a resolute force."

The kingdom has made similar offers in the past, although few have responded. But it has never made such a gesture with quite the same emphasis.

Saudi experts saw the move as a quick follow-up to the success the security forces had last week in killing or capturing major members of the most violent cell linked to Al Qaeda in the country within hours of its announcement that it had beheaded Paul M. Johnson Jr., its American hostage.

With the cell's most effective leaders eliminated, the amnesty is designed to divest the insurgent underground of its younger members and new recruits, these experts believe. The targets of the amnesty, the experts say, are those who have not yet shed blood and who might be tempted to change their ways.

There are many new and young recruits who have not yet been implicated and it is those individuals who can evidently turn themselves in and who the state is aiming at with its pardon," said Abdel Rahman Lahem, a lawyer and expert on Islamic extremists.

"The others who are directly and hugely implicated in criminal acts I don't think would give themselves up," he said. "These groups are motivated by very strong convictions and they don't even acknowledge the legitimacy of the state in the first place."

Until last weekend, many Saudis and foreigners living here felt that the kingdom was lurching out of control, in view of eight attacks in rapid succession that left some fifty people dead. But the sudden decimation of such a major terrorist cell has given much of the country, not least the royal family, the sense that the terrorist threat, while not eliminated, is manageable.

"We are still here despite the fact that every ten years we have the same question: 'Will the royal family survive?" Prince Saud al-Faisal, the foreign minister, told a small group of reporters on Wednesday. "We keep proving resilient in that."

The royal family, he added, "represents something of significance for the unity of this country, which should not be forgotten."

Still, the threat of instability has not disappeared entirely, with more than a dozen men on the government's most-wanted list still at large.

In Riyadh over the past five days, security forces have continued pressing their searches, sealing off entire neighborhoods and checking the occupants of individual houses as helicopters hovered overhead looking for anyone trying to flee. They also have yet to locate the body of Mr. Johnson—and may be unable to do so, given that the four men who are believed to have kidnapped him were all shot dead.

Another twelve men were captured, and Saudi news reports have suggested that two or three of them were on the original most-wanted list of twenty-six suspects published late last year. Of those, one surrendered and nine have been killed, leaving some sixteen whose fate is not publicly known. The Saudi government does not always make public the names of those it detains.

Those sixteen are not all among the most important terrorists in the country, Saudi and Western experts point out. Although much about their lives remains unknown, the men, who range in age from around twenty to almost forty, break down into three main categories, the experts say.

Three of them are religious sheiks who are believed to provide the Islamic justifications for violence. At least two more are experienced fighters who might take over mission planning for the group that calls itself Al Qaeda on the Arabian Peninsula, because the most-wanted member of the group, Abdelaziz al-Muqrin, died last Friday. The remainder are said to be foot soldiers for the Qaeda group about whom little is known.

Preliminary attention focused on Saleh al-Awfi, a 33-year-old former Saudi prison guard and veteran of Islamic militant groups' training camps in Afghanistan. Many believe he is the most likely the new leader of the group. He also has a penchant for writing colloquial poetry about their exploits. A second is Rakan al-Saikan, one of many men whose names are sometimes linked to the 2000 attack on the American destroyer Cole in Yemen. He may have been one of those captured last week, Saudi officials said.

Faris al-Zahrani, 27, is considered the most prominent and dangerous of the religious scholars. Mr. Zahrani wrote a book justifying the killing of Saudi police officers. There are persistent rumors that he was among those captured last week after being shot in the leg.

Another religious sheik is Abdullah al-Rashoud, who spoke out vociferously about the government's recent removal of the administration of girls' education from the religious authority.

Two of those on the list are Moroccans—Karim al-Miati and Hussein al-Huski. Mr. Miati is an explosives expert, but Mr. Huski remains a mysterious figure.

There are believed to be some 2,000 members of Al Qaeda who have worked in the kingdom in recent years, with some 350 of them being really active and the rest supporters willing to provide logistics or other help, one expert said.

Between 1,000 and 1,200 are in jail, he added, with many of the rest either on the run or gone to Iraq or elsewhere to take up holy war against the West. Recent news reports noted that the threatening tapes made by violent insurgent groups in Iraq have included the voice of at least one speaker with a Saudi accent.

The majority on the list of most-wanted suspects are from Suweidi, a poor Riyadh neighborhood where a BBC cameraman was shot dead and a correspondent critically wounded early this month. Western reporters no longer go there.

Saudi reporters describe it as an ultraconservative place, where barbers refuse to shave customers because they believe that the Prophet Muhammad ordained that all men must grow beards. Tailors there will not sew long thobes—the robes worn by Saudi men—insisting only on the above-the-ankle type that is believed to have been prevalent in Muhammad's era.

In addition, the newsstands will not sell newspapers considered too secular. For example, religious conservatives denounce the Saudi paper *Al Watan* (The Nation), calling it *Al Wathan* (The Idol). Similarly, they refer to *Al Sharq Al Awsat* (the Middle East) as *Al Shar Al Awsak* (the Dirtiest Evil).

The royal family stresses the need to isolate the insurgents from religious conservatives because their interests are different.

"First of all they don't believe in jihad and that jihad is right as the terrorists claim it to be," Prince Saud said, adding, "their objective is not to create a greater Muslim state, as Al Qaeda's is."

ENDNOTE

1. From the *New York Times,* June 24, 2004, reprinted with permission.

CHAPTER 26
Saudis Gave U.S. Extensive War Aid

John Solomon

WASHINGTON—During the Iraq war, Saudi Arabia secretly helped the United States far more than has been acknowledged, allowing operations from at least three air bases, permitting special forces to stage attacks from Saudi soil and providing cheap fuel, U.S. and Saudi officials say.

The American air campaign against Iraq was essentially managed from inside Saudi borders, where military commanders operated an air command center and launched refueling tankers, F-16 fighter jets, and sophisticated intelligence gathering flights, according to the officials.

Much of the assistance has been kept quiet for more than a year by both countries for fear it would add to instability inside the kingdom. Many Saudis oppose the war and U.S. presence on Saudi soil has been used by Osama bin Laden to build his terror movement.

But senior political and military officials from both countries told the Associated Press the Saudi royal family permitted widespread military operations to be staged from inside the kingdom during the coalition force's invasion of Iraq.

These officials would talk only on condition of anonymity because of the diplomatic sensitivity and the fact that some operational details remain classified.

Although the ground attack came from Kuwait, thousands of special forces soldiers were permitted to stage their operations into Iraq from inside Saudi Arabia, the officials said. These staging areas became essential once Turkey declined to allow U.S. forces to operate from its soil.

In addition, U.S. and coalition aircraft launched attacks, reconnaissance flights, and intelligence missions from three Saudi air bases, not just the Prince Sultan Air Base where U.S. officials have acknowledged activity.

Between 250 and 300 Air Force planes staged from Saudi Arabia, including AWACS, C-130s, refueling tankers, and F-16 fighter jets during the height of the war, the officials said.

Air and military operations during the war were permitted at the Tabuk Air Base and Arar Regional Airport near the Iraq border, the officials said.

Saudis also agreed to permit search-and-rescue missions to take off from their soil, the officials said.

Gen. T. Michael Moseley, a top Air Force general who was a key architect of the air campaign in Iraq, called the Saudis "wonderful partners," although he agreed to discuss their help only in general terms.

"We operated the command center at Saudi Arabia. We operated airplanes out of Saudi Arabia as well as sensors, and tankers," said Moseley in an interview with the AP.

He said he treasures "their counsel, their mentoring, their leadership and their support." Publicly, American and Saudi officials have portrayed the U.S. military presence during the war as minimal and limited to Prince Sultan Air Base, where Americans have operated on and off over the last decade. Any other American presence during the war was generally described as humanitarian, such as food drops, or as protection against Scud missile attacks.

PART FOUR
SAUDI GOVERNMENT INFORMATION

CHAPTER 27
Security and Human Rights
(Official Document from the Kingdom of Saudi Arabia)

All citizens in the kingdom of Saudi Arabia are Muslims and see Islam as a religion unifying them, the glory of their glories, and the guarantor of their future. The Islamic Sharee'ah law calls for the unity of society; it protects its entity and provides the methods of achieving security and safety. It is also a means of dealing with crime in all of its forms with its provisions and controls in order to protect society from the effects and dangers of criminal behavior. The Sharee'ah calls for good manners, obligations, and proper behavior founded on the power of the relation between man and his God and between people. It also breeds the inward belief and motivation for moral conduct.

The days before the foundation of the kingdom of Saudi Arabia were full of fear and fighting between tribes for trivial reasons. When King Abdel Aziz came to power [see Introduction] and unified the different regions of the country under the flag of Islam, security was reinstated and people were reassured of their lives and properties. For these reasons whoever cares to compare the past, which was full of fear and fright, with the present which is full of security and well-being, will agree with the necessity to maintain the great gains under the present system.

The Ministry of the Interior [the most important Ministry in the government] in the kingdom of Saudi Arabia, through its experiences, learned that Saudi society's kindness and abidance to good manners as well as tolerance to other ways of thinking may tempt those with ill intentions to exploit this type of calmness in order to obtain quick personal gains. This negative attitude has always been the course taken by criminals as their selfishness grows in their path to trespass [against] others. Thus, the Ministry of the Interior organized itself, laid down developing plans for its security departments, established colleges and institutes to qualify security men, and doubled the technical and human capabilities of its departments. These moves are in addition to providing citizens with technological equipment and advanced means which assist in the quick disclosure of crime and the immediate detention of criminals.

From time to time, the Ministry of Interior publicly announces the criminal acts committed by citizens or even by expatriates. Among these crimes, there are some completely new to our society, such as holdups and kidnappings of children in return for ransoms. However, it didn't take long before the criminals learned the severe punishments allotted by an efficient legal system. This system guarantees justice and equality for all. Also, from time to time, the Ministry of Interior applies punishments for crimes, which Sharee'ah condemns with deterring sentences, such as execution in retribution for capital crime or a high penalty in response to premeditated murder or to trespassing the security of society by force, violence, terrorism, or narcotics.

Reference should be made to the fact that the judiciary system in the kingdom of Saudi Arabia takes place from the general and urgent courts to the cassation body, up to the higher judicial council. Under this system, the evaluation of punishments and penalties is done by three judges in the general and urgent court. Then five judges from the cassations court look at the verdict, and then submit it to the Higher Judicial Council, the highest judiciary authority in the country, which ratifies and affirms the verdict before submission to the king for final approval. This system guarantees the sentenced person the right to plea the verdict.

The prosecution and investigation body, affiliated to the Interior Ministry, assists the judges by conducting an investigation, scrutinizing the evidence available, and taking investigative action to expose the truth. Then, it institutes the general proceedings: the procedure before the judiciary. It also supervises the execution of sentences, monitors and inspects prisons and detention stations, and assists innocent defendants.

The emphasis on evidence is a basic principle of the Islamic law. The verdict is not issued unless accurate scrutinizing and review is conducted, and, on top of that, the utmost precautions are observed before execution of the sentence.

The enforcement of Islamic Criminal Law aims at protecting the five necessities of man which are securing his soul, mind, religion, money, and honor. Any transgression [against] any of these five necessities will be met with the relevant prescribed punishment according to Islamic law. Islam stipulated that, whoever kills a soul without any right is like one who kills all people, and whoever gives life to one soul is like one who gives life to all people. Retribution is the fair sentence which gives relief to the relatives of the victim and, at the same time, it is the perfect means to ensure the protection of a person's life. The strange thing is that one finds people who sympathize with the murderer without thinking how remorseless and merciless the crime might have been.

Everybody knows well the effects of narcotics in destroying the mind and the health of people as well as its social and economic repercussions. This reality has made many governments around the world decide in favor of the death penalty on drug traffickers. What happens if a drug trafficker is not sentenced to death? Events have proven that the drug trafficker returns to his misdeeds despite security hindrances and punishments. Then, there is no way to weed out this defect, evil to society, but with execution of the criminal. At the same time, this type of punishment deters anyone from being involved in drug trafficking. The Sharee'ah also involves cutting off the hand of someone who repeatedly steals as a means to protect private and public property.

This punishment takes place after giving the thief a chance to reform himself by applying lesser penalties as a warning. His hand is not cut off, unless all attempts to reform him fail. The theory behind this punishment is that some people are not deterred by leniency and preaching, but only through severe punitive action. The punishments prescribed by Islam are not the legislation of mankind, but it is a heavenly legislation and law, laid down by the great Creator because of His wisdom, fairness, and mercy on his creatures in order for people to live in safety and peace. Allah [God], to whom all perfection and majesty are ascribed, knows well his creatures' affairs in their worldly tendencies and base instincts. This kind of approach, deemed by some people as severe to criminals, is the heavenly fair retribution that must be conducted to handle defects and crimes which threaten security and safety of society.

Application of the Islamic law (Sharee'ah) in the kingdom of Saudi Arabia has proven efficient in fighting and in lowering the crime rate. A year or two will pass in the country without hearing of anyone's hand being cut off for stealing. The number of those who had their hands cut off in the last half a century cannot be compared to the number of thieves' victims and security men killed in one year in many Western cities. Data and statistical information released in the kingdom of Saudi Arabia and abroad show that the crime rate in the kingdom is much lower than that of other countries.

Democracy

Among the fundamentals of democracy is the right of peoples to self-determination. Every country in the world rules itself in its own special way. The oldest and most famous definition of democracy is "rule of the people by the people and for the people," [as in the U.S., for example] but the ways of representing people and selecting rulers are clearly different throughout the democracies of the world. Thus, it is hard to determine the standard democratic model.

It is natural that the ruling system and the selection of representatives of the people reflect the circumstances and the nature of that people. It might not be totally suitable to apply a system that works in one country in another. Then, one must recognize the circumstances and the nature of the Saudi people in order to determine the characteristics of the pertinent system.

Saudi Arabia has an ancient Arab Muslim society with a cultural heritage that spans thousands of years. From this land, the message of Prophet Mohamed, peace be upon him, came as a mercy to mankind. Saudi Arabia has a consistent society with clear ties to its land, its Islamic religion, and its Arabic language.

This society is governed by moral principles taken from Islam, which ordains moral conduct. Saudi moral values are based on truthfulness, generosity, courage, assistance to others, observing the rights of the neighbor, relieving the grieved, and responding to he who seeks refuge.

Someone may ask, "How are the country's affairs run? Is there a constitution, is there an electoral system?" To answer these questions, a very important matter must be mentioned, namely that the ruling in Islam is Allah's ruling and the ruler is only Allah's Caliph on earth governing with Allah's ruling and applying his Sharee'ah. This is what takes place in the kingdom of Saudi Arabia. The ruler and the ruled have committed themselves to the rulings of the Qura'an and to the Prophetic Sunnah. Consequently, the consultation (*shura*) means conducting deliberations among the intelligentsia, scholars, and authorities, in order to exchange opinions and review the best possible decision for the nation's interest within the guidelines of Islamic law (Sharee'ah).

Since the first days of founding the kingdom of Saudi Arabia, King Abdel Aziz adopted the principle of consultation (shura). He formed the first consultative (shura) council in the year 1346 H [1927], five years before the declaration of the kingdom's unification. Following this example, the Custodian of the Two Holy Mosques, King Fahad Bin Abdel Aziz Al Saud, issued the basic system of government, the statute of the Consultative (shura) Council and the Areas' System on 27/8/1412H [1993]. These were followed by the Ministers' Council system on 3/3/1414H [1995], which came to represent a characteristic move in the administration of the country.

The Council consisted of a chairman and 120 members. Membership in the council was by selection of the experienced and specialized people. The council probes the systems, conventions, agreements, privileges, and other topics and proposes systems and laws with the people's and the country's interest in mind. In addition, the thirteen area councils in the country involve another aspect of the popular participation in decision-making, especially in relation to internal developmental affairs. The council of each area consists of the area prince (as a chairman), his deputy (as the deputy chairman), the deputy of the principality, government department heads in the area, and at least ten of the experienced and specialized people residing in the area.

The kingdom of Saudi Arabia is distinguished for its open door policy, which means opening the door to citizens to meet the king, the crown prince, top officials, princes, and ministers in order to submit to them their complaints and requests. If the top official cannot provide an immediate answer, then the citizen's request is quickly forwarded to the permit department to settle it as soon as possible. During specific times reception rooms are opened for the citizens to meet the king, the crown prince, and areas' princes to sit in order to put forward their concerns. This fully democratic tradition is ancient, and it suits Saudis more and guarantees the dignity and the interest of its people. It is a unique Saudi method, not borrowed from any other system or country and not imposed on the people. Thus, the kingdom of Saudi Arabia practices democracy in this unique manner.

Human Rights

First of all, we must explain that Islam grants men his basic human rights unprecedented in any other system. Man, as stipulated by the Islamic law (Sharee'ah), is absolutely the best of Allah's creatures. Allah blessed him with reason, and determined his rights and duties that guarantee his happiness in this life and in the hereafter. Allah detailed this sufficiently. The kingdom of Saudi Arabia came second to none of the Islamic countries to show its reservations to a few of the articles of the International Declaration of Human Rights, approved by the United Nations in 1948.

Islam considers human rights the responsibility of individual and of society. This issue is not mere moral preaching. Human rights in Isla m include positive aspects that are not mentioned in the International Declaration of Human Rights; moreover, the declaration contained articles contradicting the Islamic law (Sharee'ah). For this reason, the kingdom of Saudi Arabia had its reservations about it. This stance was also taken against the International Charter for the Economic, Social, and Cultural Rights, released by the United Nations, which contained articles in contradiction with Islam. On the one hand, human rights as treated by the Islamic law (Sharee'ah) are superior to what is stated by the United Nations. On the other hand, the United Nations' human rights are laid down by people who drew them from their present societies without recognizing that there is a large Muslim society that adopts the legislation of Allah and rejects what contradicts it. The kingdom has worked hard to promote the human rights declaration of Islam, which was issued by the Islamic Conference Organization on 13/1/1411 [4/8/1990] and is known as the Cairo Declaration.

The Saudi Ministry of Foreign Affairs explained the kingdom of Saudi Arabia's stance toward the International Declaration of Human Rights and the International Charter for Economic, Social, and Cultural Rights in the proper time. The ministry also showed the merits of human rights in Islam such as accuracy, excellence, and totality. Among these merits are:

A. The dignity of man and honoring him via the Holy Qura'an verses.

B. Setting no differences in dignity and the basic rights of all men.

C. The unity of the family and that the best man is he who is most beneficent to his family.

D. The calling for making acquaintance, cooperation, and presenting all types of benevolence to all mankind.

E. The freedom of religion and the rejection of compulsion by Islam.

F. Barring aggression on man's money, blood, and honor.

G. Vouching for each other in the Islamic society and the right of man to a good life. Freeing man from the chains of need and poverty by requesting a known rightful portion of money from the rich to be given to the needy.

H. Punishing those who refrain from learning or teaching the principles of Islam. This right is not found in any other legislation.

Naturally, everything relative to human rights is applied in the kingdom of Saudi Arabia since its foundation. This application is represented in laws and systems issued by the state and applied by government departments. Each of them takes over a part of the responsibilities of life. This incorporates human rights for which the government national organizations and departments are set up and join forces in order to apply the law of Allah and crystallize its merits through praxis.

Human rights in the kingdom of Saudi Arabia are based on the principle of the dignity of man and his right to freedom, knowledge, and work in order to lead a noble and dignified life in accordance with the fair and wise provisions of Islamic law (Sharee'ah).

[Editor's note: Chapters 27–32 are official documents from the Ministry of Interior, Royal Government of Saudi Arabia; all translations are theirs with only minor grammatical changes by the editor.]

CHAPTER 28
The System of Government
(Official Document from the Kingdom of Saudi Arabia)

The kingdom of Saudi Arabia is an Arab Islamic sovereign state. Its religion is Islam, its constitution is the Holy Quran and the prophetic sunnah, and its language is Arabic. The government of the kingdom of Saudi Arabia draws its power from the book of Allah [God] and the tradition of Allah's messenger which are its primary sources and all the systems of the state. The basis of the ruling system in the kingdom is justice, shura and quality according to the Islamic law (Sharee'ah system). This system was laid down within other articles of the basic system of government of the kingdom of Saudi Arabia which was issued together with the Shura council and Areas' System on 27-7-1412, corresponding to 1/3/1993.

The Custodian of the two holy mosques, King Fahd bin Abdel Aziz Al Saud [1982 to the present], addressed the citizens, summing up the identity of the kingdom, the source of its legitimacy, and the political practice of its government, which was based, since the state's establishment, on a stable and clear-cut concept. This concept was laid down by the kingdom's founder, King Abdel Aziz Al Saud. During his reign, and because of the development of modern life, it became necessary that political systems emanate from this concept of government. After his death, his sons contributed in modernizing and developing this country. The relationship between the citizens and their rulers is based on fixed foundations and ancient traditions of love, mutual mercifulness, interchangeable respect, and loyalty stemming from free contentment deep-rooted in the conscience of the people of this country throughout consecutive generations. This relationship is practiced through an ancient tradition of easy access to the government offices by all people. Thus, it is not strange that this system clearly states that the Council of the king and the Council of the crown prince are open for every citizen and for everyone who has a complaint or grievance.

The issuance of the system was an expression of the Saudi leadership in continuing its development according to the tolerant Islamic law (Sharee'ah) upon which the first Saudi state was founded more than two and a half centuries ago. This was when its founder Imam Mohamed Bin Saud and the reformer shiekh [sic] Mohamed Bin Abdel Wahab pledged [to] strive for the elevation of Allah's word, apply Allah's Sharee'ah and defend the Islamic creed. [See Introduction.] The kingdom of Saudi Arabia's fulfillment of Islam as a creed and its Sharee'ah continued, and its people were satisfied with the Islamic law when they applied it in their life and all their affairs. This fulfillment was reflected in the kingdom's political. [sic] Which was incarnated in the security and stability which the country witnessed and in its overall development. This course was also represented in the kingdom's persistent efforts to unify Arabs and Muslims word and care for their solidarity in addition to exerting all efforts for their well-being. Events and episodes proved the kingdom's faithful stances and fulfillment of its obligations toward the Arab and the Islamic nation, and its other international obligations. As a result, the kingdom gained respect of the international community for its role and prestige as well as for its wise leadership.

The basic political system of ruling is very detailed and inclusive of the ruling mechanisms; the transfer of leadership between the ruling and the ruled; the nature of the state's judiciary, executive, and organizational authorities' functions; the state's rights and duties; and the rights of citizens. There is always update [sic] of previous systems which coincided with the tremendous development of the kingdom on a large scope in various areas.

The Shura Council

The establishment of the Shura Council as commanded by Islam is considered one of the pillars upon which the kingdom of Saudi Arabia was founded. The concept of Shura in Islam means reaching consensus based on mutual counseling and this is not a political doctrine but a fixed foundation of Islamic society.

When King Abdel Aziz proclaimed the unification of the country, the Consultative Shura Council was one of the first and most important achievements of the king. He issued his order in the year 1346H [1927] to form the first Consultative Council. The first one to preside over the Consultative Council was Prince Faisal Bin Abel Aziz, deputy of the king in the Hegaz region. Later Prince Faisal became the king. At the beginning, the Council consisted of eight members. Its number reached twenty members in the year 1372H [1952]. The Council held its sessions daily and in the year 1375H [1955]. King Saud released a royal order to raise to twenty-five the number of members of the Consultative Shura Council and to hold its sessions weekly. After the issuance of the cabinet system in the year 1373H [1953], the cabinet took over the Consultative Shura Council prerogatives. This went on until royal order No. A/91, dated 27/8/1412H [1991], was issued to put into effect the new Consultative Council system. Later, the internal regulations and rules organizing the council's work were issued in accordance with royal order Number 1/15, dated 3/3/1414 [1993]. The regulations included 62 articles in six chapters comprising everything relative to the council's work and its members' rights, obligations, and responsibilities. The council consisted of a chairman and sixty members to whom thirty other members were added on 3/31418 (7 July 1997) in agreement with the royal order. The council, for the second term, was formed of ninety members and according to its system, the period of membership was limited to four years. When forming the council anew, it is to be borne in mind that the number of its new members is not less than half the number of its current members. Furthermore, the headquarters of the council is in Riyadh and the council can meet in another region of the kingdom if the king deems it necessary. The council is to hold an ordinary session every two weeks at least and the chairman of the council has the right to advance or postpone its time together with the right to hold an emergency session to discuss a specific topic.

The council started its agenda in its headquarters in Riyadh after the Custodian of the Two Holy Mosques inaugurated it on 16/7/1414H [29/12/1993]. Its first session was held on 20/7/1414H corresponding to 2 January 1994 with the attendance of its chairman, secretary general and the sixty members who were selected from those experienced, efficient, and highly qualified people. Eight specialized committees were formed whose work included the following fields: Islamic affairs, foreign affairs, services and facilities affairs, administrative and systems affairs, security affairs, educational and cultural affairs, and media affairs. These committees were assisted by an integrated body in whose administration several national experienced and efficient people worked.

At the time of forming the committees and naming a chairman, a deputy chairman, and the members of each committee, the council started its work dealing with the topics forwarded to it in the framework of its special ties and tasks as outlined in its system and mentioned in the fifteenth article of its system.

These are:

A. Discussion of the general plan for economic and social development and giving opinions.
B. Studying the systems, regulations, international conventions, agreements, and privileges and proposing relevant ideas.
C. Explaining the systems.
D. Discussing the annual reports submitted by the ministries and the other government bodies and proposing relevant ideas.

Since its foundation the council witnessed an intensive activity. Its chairman received a number of Consultative Council members, Parliamentary delegations, and ambassadors to the kingdom from Arab, Islamic, and friendly countries. Moreover, the chairman, accompanied by official delegations comprising a number of the council members, visited many Arab, Islamic, and friendly countries in order to support diplomatic relations and to promote cooperation between the kingdom and the other countries.

The Cabinet System

The cabinet in the kingdom of Saudi Arabia was founded through a royal order signed by King Abdel Aziz, may Allah bless his soul, in the year 1373 [October 1953] before his death. The cabinet system began work that same year. Before that date, the administration of the state was based on a system issued in the year 1350 [December 1931] in which the king took care of state affairs with the aid of his ministers, advisors, experienced and specialized people together with the Shura Council.

Development of the cabinet and its committees' work methods continued under the reign of King Saud, King Faisal, King Khalid and then in the reign of the Custodian of the Two Holy Mosques who issued the new cabinet system via royal decree No A/13, dated 3/3/1414 [20 August 1993] which replaces the system created in the year 1373 H and its amendments. Under the new system, the cabinet takes over laying down the internal, foreign, financial, economic, educational and defense policies and all the general affairs of the state. The cabinet also supervises the execution of all these policies and reviews the Shura Council's resolutions. This policy represents the font of reference for the financial and administrative affairs of the ministries and the other government departments.

The new cabinet system stated the period of service for the ministers and for other high positions, which are determined by royal appointment, to be four years. This new system also stated that the cabinet is to be reshuffled with a royal order. The reshuffling of the cabinet will be the responsibility of the following three departments: the cabinet divan, the cabinet general secretariat, and the organization of experts.

The king assumes the chairmanship of the cabinet and directs the general policy of the state. He also guarantees direction, coordination, and cooperation among the government's various departments. In addition, he guarantees consistence, continuity, and unity in the cabinet agenda and supervises the cabinet, ministries, and the government departments together with monitoring the systems, regulations, and resolutions.

The System of the Areas

The system of the areas, which was issued via a royal decree on 27/7/1412 H and amended by a royal decree on 20/3/1414, aims at elevating the level of administrative work and of development in the kingdom. It also aims at observing security and discipline, and it guarantees citizens' rights and freedoms under Islamic codes. When dividing the administrative regions, residential, geographical, security, environmental, and transportation considerations were borne in mind. As a result, the administrative regions in the kingdom were divided into the following thirteen regions: Riyadh, Makkah, Madinah, Quassim, the eastern, Assir, Tabuk, Hail, the northern borders, Jizan, Najran, Baha, and Jouf. Every prince, who is in the same rank as a minister, takes over the administration of each area according to the general policy of the state. The system clearly and accurately determined the tasks assigned each prince. It also stated that the appointed princes and their deputies are responsible before the Minister of the Interior who has the right to recommend their appointment or dismissal. Among the reforms which the system contained is the introduction of a council for each area consisting of its prince as a chairman, his deputy to the deputy of this council, the principality deputy, and government departments' heads of each area. The appointments are determined by a resolution from the cabinet according to a recommendation from the Minister of the Interior, and a number of citizens amounting to no fewer than ten. These citizens must be people of knowledge, experience, and specialty and are appointed by an order from the Premier based on the candidature of the area prince and the approval of the Minister of Interior provided that their membership be under a renewable period of four years. Through these systems and legislation, the formation of both the state's executive and the organizational powers are confined to a period of time followed by renewal or appointment. This means creating a characteristic move in the ruling method and I [sic] the administration of the kingdom as contained in the resolution of the Custodian of the Two Holy Mosques concerned with the new shuffling of the cabinet in the third month of the year 1420 [1999]. The point is to allow new people into many major organizations of the state, such as universities and public bodies.

[*Note:* Saudi Arabia uses a dual dating system: the first numbers refer to the ancient Islamic system of dates and the second system follows the Western European system where day, month and year are listed in that order.]

CHAPTER 29
Education
(Official Document from the Kingdom of Saudi Arabia)

The kingdom of Saudi Arabia is witnessing an overall educational boom which is represented in eight universities whose campuses, regulations, and scientific equipment match those in the most advanced universities in the world. This boom is also manifested in thousands of elementary, preparatory, and secondary schools for boys and girls in addition to the specialized institutes and colleges in the various branches of science and schools for old people and kindergartens.

This growth is the fruit of the continuous efforts started by King Abdel Aziz, the founder of the kingdom of Saudi Arabia, since the early years of the kingdom and have been looked after by his sons after him (kings of the kingdom). The maximum development has been achieved during the period of the Custodian of the Two Holy Mosques, King Fahad Ibn Abdel Aziz, who has given special care to education since the time he was the first Minister of Education in the kingdom's history when this Ministry was established in 1953. The kingdom has achieved quick leaps in education. The following figures sum up the educational achievements from 1970 to 1999:

— The total number of schools for all stages has increased from 3,283 schools to more than 23,000 schools. During this period, the educational organizations have increased about seven times.

— Those joining the educational organizations have increased from 600,000 students to 4.7 million students (boys and girls). The number has increased eight times.

— The number of students in higher education has increased from 8,000 to more than 360,000 (young men and women).

— The number of students in technical schools and institutes has increased from 840 to more than 38,000.

— The number of students in vocational training centers has increased from 578 to around 10,000.

During the same time period the average opening of schools is as follows:

One elementary school every day.

One preparatory school every two days.

One secondary school every five days.

Since 1970 the government has prioritized the development of human resources and manpower training as one of its main targets for the five-year development plans. During the sixth five-year plan covering the period from 1995 to 2000, the total amount allocated for education was 183.4 billion Saudi riyals; that is, 21.5 percent of the amount approved for this plan. In this fiscal year 1420-1421 (2000), the budget for education and manpower training is more than 49 billion Saudi riyals; i.e., 26 percent of the general budget of the kingdom.

The number of boy schools being supervised by the Ministry of Education in 1419H (1998) is 12,323 schools accommodating a total of 2,171,010 students and 157,128 teachers, while the number of girl schools under the supervision of the General Presidency for Girls' Education is 13,598 schools accommodating 2,223,382 students and 200,303 teachers. Official statistics indicate that the eight universities of the kingdom in addition to teacher colleges, health colleges, and other colleges include 250 colleges accommodating more than 360,000 students (young men and women) in the bachelor stage only and around 17,000 teaching staff members. The number of education units belonging to the General Organization for Technical Education and Vocational Training is around seventy-six units, such as technical colleges, Industrial Secondary Institutes, Commercial Secondary Institutes, Agricultural Secondary Institutes, Technical Inspector Institutes, in addition to the Trainers' Preparation Institute, and Aids Center. All of these technical and vocational schools accommodate more than 38,000 students. There are as well vocational training centers (thirty centers), which work two shifts, morning and evening classes, and accommodate around 10,000 trainees in various crafts.

The General Organization for Technical Education and Vocational Training supervises the private sector training centers (more than 300) Institutes as well as training centers accommodating more than 18,000 students. As an extension of the state's care for special education, 118 institutes have been built for boys and twenty-five for girls to look after the handicapped (blind, deaf, dumb, and retarded) to prepare and qualify them to use their remaining senses in order to be active members of society. Whereas the boy institutes belonging to the Ministry of Education accommodate around 7,600 students with more than 1,834 teachers, the girl institutes belonging to the General Presidency for Girls' Education accommodate around 3,400 students with 1,980 teachers.

In addition to free education in all government schools, the state grants financial allowances for students (boys and girls) in some educational levels, which reach to one thousand riyals monthly in some colleges, technical colleges, and specialized institutes, in addition to health care, housing, food, and transportation in many cases. Besides the state's educational organizations, the private sector runs and operates many schools in various stages starting from kindergartens to the secondary level. The Ministry of Education and the General Presidency for Girls' Education supervise these schools, support them, and provide them with school curricula, syllabi, and educational aid.

The spread of education in various stages and levels and the efforts exerted by the state through the evening schools for the elimination of illiteracy and for the increase in teaching facilities have had clear effects in reducing the illiteracy among men and women. The number of this type of school under the supervision of the Ministry of Education in the school year 1419H-1420H (1999) is 1,155 schools accommodating 35,168 students, while the number of schools under the supervision of the General Presidency for Girls Education is 2,107 schools accommodating 74,648 students. The kingdom of Saudi Arabia has been congratulated by international and regional organizations which granted it four awards in appreciation for the country's efforts in eliminating social and job illiteracy. In 1996 the kingdom represented by the Culture and Education Department of the Ministry of Defense and Aviation got an award from UNESCO. The kingdom represented by the Secretariat General for adult learning through the Ministry of Education got a prize from the Arab Organization for Education, Culture and Science for eliminating the social and job illiteracy. In 1998 kingdom represented by the General Presidency for Girls' Education got a NOMA prize which is granted by UNESCO. In 1999 the kingdom represented by the National Guard Deputyship for Cultural and Educational Affairs got the International Council for Adult Learning prize which is granted by the International Council for Adult Learning in Canada.

CHAPTER 30
Health and Social Care

(Official Government Document from the Kingdom of Saudi Arabia)

The kingdom of Saudi Arabia adopts ambitious policies in the field of health and social care and provides the highest level of medical services to its people and pilgrims during the pilgrimage *(Hajj)* season. Some of the kingdom's hospitals and specialized medical centers achieved tangible successes in the fields of advanced surgeries, such as organ transplants and other accurate operations done by Saudi physicians.

The state, represented by the Ministry of Labor and Social Affairs, pays great attention to social care programs for the citizens in need, especially those whose social, psychological, or physical circumstances prevent them from adapting to society. These programs provide them with sound upbringing, preparations, and rehabilitation, and help them with overcoming their social conditions.

Health Services

The kingdom's government works, through the Ministry of Health, to make available the health services in all parts of the kingdom. Some other government departments, such as the Ministry of Defense, the Presidency of the National Guard, the Interior Ministry, the Ministry of Education, the General Presidency for Girls' Education, the General Presidency for Youth and the General Organization for Social Insurance, make available health services for their employees and their families in the hospitals and medical centers established by these departments. The medical services in the kingdom, besides their quality, are free of charge. Some hospitals, affiliated to the military sectors, gained world recognition due to their excellence in every sense of the word.

In addition to its supervision on the health sector, the Ministry of Health follows up conditions of the citizens sent abroad for treatment, whose number has shrunk in the last few years as a result of the development of the medical sector inside the kingdom.

The Ministry of Health cared for preparing and qualifying medical cadres as it established forty-four institutes for males and females and developed these institutes by turning them into colleges. Medical studies started in thirteen medical science colleges in a number of cities in the kingdom. This is in addition to nine medical colleges affiliated to the Saudi universities. On the other hand, the Saudi Red Crescent Society, which was founded in 1963, provides medical aid services and participates during the pilgrimage season. The society has eleven branches to which 155 centers are affiliated. More than 2,791 persons work in the society, ranging from physicians and pharmacists to first aid personnel, and it has about 648 ambulances.

The following are some indicators which reflect factual data of the health services in the kingdom:

— In the year 1997, the number of hospitals in the kingdom reached 303 hospitals, 180 of which are affiliated to the Ministry of Health, eighty-four are affiliated to the private sector, having made use of the support of the government that offered loans to the tune of fifty percent of the cost of construction and equipping. The other hospitals are affiliated to the other government bodies. These hospitals support primary health care centers, which number 2,348 [with] 1,737 affiliated to the Ministry of Health.

— The number of beds in all hospitals in the kingdom rose to 44,213 and the rate of the number of beds in proportion to the number of inhabitants became 234 beds for every one thousand people.

— The number of physicians in all health sectors in the kingdom reached 31,585 physicians. The number of the nursing body numbers 62,899 nurses and the number of aiding people reached 35,227 assistants. The number of physicians against the population became one physician for every 6.1 persons. There are a number of specialized hospitals in the kingdom, such as King Faisal Special Hospital in Riyadh, which comprises a medical research center and another center for cancer research, and the King Khalid specialized ophthalmology hospital. These hospitals take over the treatment of serious cases referred to them from the public hospitals.

— Among the specialized centers established in the kingdom is the Saudi Center for Organ Transplanting. Since its establishment in 1987 and up to the end of December 1997, it supervised the transplanting of 2,299 kidneys, 144 livers, 75 hearts and 7,743 corneas. Also 132 heart valves were used.

— Currently, work is under way to inaugurate King Fahad medical city in Riyadh whose construction is completed. It contains a public hospital with a capacity of 459 beds, a children's hospital with a capacity of 246 beds, a confinement hospital with a capacity of 236 beds, a kidney and medical rehabilitation center, and a hospital for mental health outside Riyadh with a capacity of 300 beds.

— The kingdom is singled out with a special sort of health care, which is medical evacuation through a fleet of airplanes equipped with medical accessories for aiding and transporting patients from their locations to hospitals. The medical evacuation fleet, which is supervised by the Armed Forces' Medical Services, comprises more than twelve planes. Many patients and injured people make use of this service annually.

— The rate of vaccination in the kingdom is one of the highest in the world as it reached 93.7 percent for tuberculosis, 94 percent for viral hepatitis, 93 percent for measles, and 95 percent for the bacterial treble [sic] and kids' paralysis.

Services of Social Development and Care

Programs of social development and care receive great interest from the state. The Ministry of Labor and Social Affairs plays a salient role in offering services of care, rehabilitation, and care for childhood, motherhood, orphans, juveniles, the disabled, and others. It makes available means of decent living for citizens who face poor social, health and economic conditions. There are also social development programs which aim at raising the economic and social level of the citizens through programs that depend on personal efforts. In addition to the services, the state offers to the above-mentioned groups, charity societies numbering 187, twenty of which are women's. They manage social institutions, programs [for] childhood care, motherhood, and kindergartens. Those societies, to which the state offers financial, technical, and administrative support, organize cultural programs for caring for the disabled and the elderly. They also organize other programs relative to the constructing and improving residences, such as the charity residence for destitute families. This is in addition to the health services and physical treatment they provide. The total revenues of the charity societies during 1998 reached SR 811.4 million, while their expenditures in the same year reached SR 622.5 million. The amount of support forwarded by the ministry to charity societies reached in 1999 SR 53.03 million. The following are some facts and information about the social development and care, supervised by the Ministry of Labor and Social Affairs [referred to hereafter as the Ministry].

— The number of social houses, affiliated to the Ministry, reached seventy-seven houses, compete with facilities and accessories.

— The Ministry cares for childhood through five social houses in major areas of the kingdom by providing the social and psychological atmosphere suitable for rearing children of special conditions, from their birth to the age of six. In these houses, educational and recreational programs are conducted to compensate for the child's lack of family.

— The Ministry cares for the orphans who turn six, both males and females. This is in addition to the children of prisoners, patients, and those who cannot work or those who lost the factors of sound social upbringing to their families. This is done through sixteen houses, eleven of which are for social education for males. They receive kids from the ages of six to twelve. The Ministry also does this through two institutions for standard social education that receive children after the age of eighteen, and three social houses for social education for girls who are received at the age of six. The houses participate in caring for and preparing them until they become house ladies, able to lead a noble family life. Each girl getting married gets a monetary grant of SR 20,000.

— The Ministry applies the "alternative care program," in which care for a number of orphans and those with special conditions is entrusted to families selected according to special social conditions. Those children are subject to the supervision and follow up [by] the ministry departments. The family, which is entrusted with caring for the child, gets a monthly aid. This aid increases in case the child joins a school. However, most of the Saudi families volunteer to embrace those children aspiring to review the rewards from Allah.

— Care for the elderly and the disabled by the Ministry is done through ten houses in which all sorts of health, psychological care, and religious, cultural, and recreational programs suitable for them are available.

— The crippled are rehabilitated through the craft rehabilitation projects and social care programs for the crippled together with their peers. There are institutions for the care of paralyzed children in Riyadh and Taif. There are also five houses for craft rehabilitation, two of which are for girls, three centers of social rehabilitation for those who are seriously crippled, and nine centers for total rehabilitation. In addition to this, the Ministry assists the families of the crippled, who want to care for kids themselves. In 1999, 45,733 cases of crippled and paralyzed children benefited from aid amounting to SR 210 million.

— The Ministry supervises the treatment of divergence of the juveniles. As for the treatment programs, they are conducted through seven houses for social observance and three institutions for girls' care. Although the Ministry takes over the social, psychological, and cultural programs, craft training programs and sports activities in these houses and institutions, the Ministry of Education and the General Presidency of Girls' Education provide the educational programs in their three stages.

— The social programs are carried out through fifteen centers for social development which serve the rural areas, seven centers for social services serving urban areas, and fifty-eight social development local committees that take over the job of the social development centers in the areas. In the administration of these centers, the Ministry of Labor and Social Affairs is aided by the Ministry of Education, the Ministry of Health, and the Ministry of Agriculture, Water, Principality, and Village Affairs.

— The Ministry participates in supporting the multipurpose cooperative societies, which number 162 working in the fields of agriculture consumption and public services.

— The social insurance represents one of the aspects of care to which the government pays attention. The Ministry Secretariat for social insurance affairs, through its main and branch offices, numbering seventy-six, conducts field research and pays to all those deserving social insurance in the form of pensions given periodically or as temporary aid. Some groups of citizens make use of this payment as they need care and aid. They are divided into two groups:

A. The pensions group: this includes orphans, those totally unable to work, and the women who have no one to provide for them.

B. The group of aid that includes those partially unable to work, families of prisoners, those plagued with individual disasters, the families deserted by their providers, the urgent and recurrent aid, and the aid for the crippled.

— The annual allotment for social insurance [was] raised in 1993 from SR 1.5 billion to 2.7 billion annually.

— These are some of the patterns of the kingdom of Saudi Arabia's attention for social care programs stemming from the teachings of Islam. These teachings urge social solidarity. This interest is incorporated in the increasing monetary allocations, which are appropriated for social purposes. These allocations have risen from SR 533 million in 1990 to 724 million in 1996.

CHAPTER 31
Agriculture
(Official Document from the Kingdom of Saudi Arabia)

The kingdom of Saudi Arabia has sought to adopt development policies that aim at attaining food security and self-sufficiency from agricultural crops and animal products, like dairy products, eggs, and meat.

Since an early stage, the kingdom has been putting this aim on the top of its priorities, which has been realized to a large extent. The first steps were taken by King Abdel Aziz when founding the kingdom. He helped his people by giving them full freedom to utilize the arable lands, by exempting the machinery from customs fees, and by distributing the machinery to the farmers to be paid on interest-free installments. King Abdel Aziz also ordered the creation of the Directorate of Agriculture in 1948 and kept it connected with the Ministry of Finance in order to improve the irrigation systems by distributing the water pumps, building the dams and canals, repairing the water springs and wells, reclaiming the agricultural land, and giving loans to farmers. After the expansion of its activities and its increasing responsibilities, the Directorate became in 1953 the Ministry of Agriculture and Water and Prince Sultan Ibn Abdel Aziz was appointed as its first Minister. Since that time, this Ministry has been devoted to making the studies and plans to boost the agricultural sectors, both in crop and animal production, in addition to developing sources of water.

It is known that the geography of the kingdom is mostly desert with severe environmental conditions in most areas in addition to shortage in water resources and rains, but thanks to Allah, the strong determination of our people, and the use of modern agricultural techniques and methods, those difficulties were overcome and the kingdom of Saudi Arabia, in a short period of time, was converted from a food-importing country to a food-producing country with net gains for the economy and its exports.

Several Incentives
The most important incentives the government has in agriculture is distributing the lands free of charge to the farmers and agricultural companies and providing aid and long-term loans

through the agricultural bank, which was established in 1962. The state pays 50 percent of the value of machines and irrigation pumps and 45 percent of the value of agricultural machines, equipment, and local and imported fertilizers. In addition, it distributes the improved seeds and seedlings for low prices, provides agricultural guidance and veterinarian services, and offers pest control services through the agricultural directorates, units, and offices all over the kingdom. The state also buys the agricultural crops from the farmers, especially wheat and barley, at preferential prices through the General Organization for Grain Silos and Flour Mills, which have existed since 1972.

Agricultural Roads

The state has been so concerned with the agricultural roads to serve farmers, facilitate their movements, and market their products in the main marketing centers, that together with the Ministry of Communication it has built agricultural roads parallel with the main roads program. The total length of the agricultural roads for 1986 was 100,000 km, while in 1970 it was only 3500 km.

Increasing the Agricultural Roads

Because of the government's support for the agricultural sector, the kingdom has witnessed the citizens' great interest in investing in agricultural fields, and the establishment of big Joint Stock Companies, which have increased the cultivated area in the kingdom from 600,000 hectares in 1980 to 1.6 million hectares in 1992. Further, 2.5 million hectares of lands have been distributed to farmers, and the Agricultural Bank has provided loans to both farmers and investors in agricultural and animal production. Until 1986 these loans amounted to 30.4 billion riyals, which helped establish more than 3,000 specialized agricultural projects for producing vegetables, fruits, dairy products, and meats. The bank also has provided aid for the product requirements (agricultural machinery, equipment, and tools), which have reached more than 11.1 billion riyals from 1973 up to the end of the fiscal year 1998.

The General Organization for Grain Silos and Flour Mills has constructed ten industrial compounds in the agricultural production regions of the kingdom for storing the grains, producing flour, and manufacturing fodder. The storage capacity of the grain silos has reached 2.38 million tons and the productivity of the flour mills has increased to 1.61 million tons annually.

Production of Wheat

The kingdom of Saudi Arabia has a leading experience in producing wheat. It reached the self-sufficiency stage in 1985 and began exporting from 1986 onwards. The highest rate of wheat production in the kingdom was in 1412 H (1992) as it reached more than 4.2 million tons. But in an effort to ration water consumption and to maintain groundwater levels, wheat production has been gradually reduced since 1413 H/1993 to reach 1.8 million tons in 1417 H/1997. Present production is for self-sufficiency purposes only, and wheat exports have been stopped. The last wheat export was in 20.12.1415 H (May 1995). A similar action has been taken to reduce the production of barley, which reached a maximum of 1,822,950 tons and has been reduced to 464,000 tons as of 1416 H/ (1996).

Vegetables and Fruits

In 1998 the kingdom's vegetable production was 2.7 million tons with some surplus, which were exported to neighboring countries. The production of fruits was 1.2 million tons, including grapes (140,000 tons) and citrus fruits, which amounted to 87,000 tons. The kingdom produced around 649,000 tons of dates annually (there are around thirteen million planted trees in the kingdom), and there are twenty-four processing plants for marketing the dates in and out of kingdom. It is a fact that the kingdom contributes large quantities of dates to the World Food Program.

Husbandry Farms and Production

In 1997 animal production in the kingdom reached 280,000 cows, about one million sheep, 626,400 goats, 750,000 camels, and 395.2 million birds. While the production of animals has increased rapidly, the dairy products have reached 883,000 tons, eggs 2,500 million, chickens 451,000 tons, red meats 157,000 tons, and fish 55,000 tons. Thus the kingdom has achieved self-sufficiency and even export potential in many agricultural products, which made the food and agricultural organization of the United Nations (FAO) award its international prize for 1997 to King Fahad in appreciation for his leading role in this field and his contribution in fighting poverty and hunger in developing countries.

High Growth Rates

The agricultural policies adopted by the kingdom of Saudi Arabia have resulted in achieving high growth rates for the agricultural development progress in the kingdom. The annual growth rate for the agricultural sectors has reached 8.4 percent during the period 1969–1996, which made the agricultural sector contribute thirty-four billion riyals to the total local revenue.

Developing Water Resources

In the field of developing water resources, the Ministry of Agriculture and Water has conducted an overall survey of the water resources in the kingdom, and has tried to supply drinking water to all cities, towns, and villages of the country; 5,500 pipe wells have been dug. Private wells have reached 103,118. Most of them are for agricultural purposes. The Ministry has achieved 1,290 projects for the supply of drinking water to towns and villages, and the Ministry operates and maintains them through the national companies and establishments. To make use of the rain and flood water, the Ministry had built until 1998 198 dams in various regions of the country with a storage capacity of about 780 million M3. As [a] strategic option, the kingdom chose to desalinate sea water in order to procure a permanent source of drinking water and to establish the General Organization for Water Desalination whose projects have become too many in a short time such that the kingdom has become the largest producer of desalinated water in the world. The desalination stations have become twenty-seven stations on the western and eastern coast of the kingdom, which supply more than forty cities and villages. These stations produce about 2.5 million cubic meters, 667 million gallons of desalinated water, daily in addition to producing 3,600 megawatts of electricity. It is expected that production will increase to three million cubic meters, 800 million gallons daily, and 5,000 megawatts of electricity after operating the new desalination stations, which are currently under construction. The quantities of water currently produced by the desalination stations cover about seventy percent of the total requirements of the main cities of the kingdom, and the electric power generated from them cover thirty percent of the electric consumption.

CHAPTER 32
The Saudi Economy

(Official Document from the Kingdom of Saudi Arabia)

The Kingdom of Saudi Arabia made huge progress in its economic march through backing its production capability in the sectors of commerce, industry, electricity, oil, agriculture, construction, contracting, and banks. The five-year development plans, started in 1970, concentrated on developing the country's infrastructure and resources in order to widen its economic base, diversify the national income, and achieve economic efficiency for both the government and private sectors. In addition, there has been a move to reinforce the role of the private sector in the national economy, to develop the much-needed manpower, to increase jobs, and to rationalize government and private expenditure.

The government of the kingdom of Saudi Arabia continues its efforts to develop its economy by offering more incentives to the private sector and maintaining the strength and stability of the Saudi currency. In this regard, the higher economic council was formed, the higher council for petroleum was reshuffled, a new system for foreign investment was released, the general organization of investment was established, and the cabinet issued a resolution to grant foreign tourist visas to the kingdom and to establish the higher organization for tourism. Among the policies of the government to increase the role of the private sector are:

— Studying the feasibility of transferring the proprietorship and administration of some governmental commercial activities to the private sector. This is in order to make the final outcome of the privatization policy positive for the government and the private sector. The kingdom has had a successful experience in this field, represented in the establishment in 1976 of the Saudi Arabian basic industries company, offering part of its shares to the public. The Saudi and the Gulf Cooperation Council Countries citizens own 25 percent of the company shares.

In this context, Saudi Telecommunications with all its facilities was converted to a joint-stock company, whose shares were put up for public subscription. In addition, some services of harbor administration and operation were turned over to the private sector, encouraging the establishment of giant joint stock companies.

— Attracting foreign companies to invest in the kingdom. The government invited large oil companies to invest in the field of natural gas and form a ministerial committee to study offers of the companies.

— Expanding the use of private capital money in financing many government projects, such as constructing schools and other projects.

— Supporting the small installations through coordination between the government's different departments and the chambers of commerce and industry in the kingdom.

Fast Leaps

The following figures reflect factual data of the Saudi economy and its fast leaps achieved despite the economic stagnation that has prevailed in the world in the last few years.

— The economic growth in the kingdom represented in its total domestic output recorded a remarkable improvement in its performance. This growth, based on the General Statistics Department estimates, reached 8.44 percent at current prices in 1999. The total domestic output at the end of the year 1419-1420H (1999) is estimated at SR 521.3 billion compared to SR 480.8 billion last year.

— The private sector participates in the total domestic output with a percentage of 38 percent at current prices and 48 percent at fixed prices. The performance of the private sector went on its improvement, most of its branches were renewed, and the industrial sector achieved, for example, a growth at a rate of 6.3 percent.

— Expectations indicate that the standard figure of the cost of living in 1999 decreased by 1.2 percent compared to last year. This percentage reflects the price stability that the domestic market has witnessed.

— The current account of the balance of payments decreased by a rate of 70.3 percent to reach SR 14.6 billion compared to SR 49.2 billion in 1998. This is attributed to the rise of oil prices in the second half of 1999. Non-oil exports are estimated to grow by a rate of 1.6 percent to reach SR 23.8 billion, while imports decreased by a ratio of 1.2 percent to reach SR 102.8 billion, which was SR 104 billion in 1996.[1]

— The Saudi industrial products are exported to markets in more than 120 countries all over the world.

— The number of factories in the kingdom reached 3,190, with a total finance of more than SR 232 billion. In these factories, about 293.7 laborers [in each factory] work up to the first quarter of 1420 H (1999).

— In addition to the two industrial cities in Jubail and Yanbu, whose planning was supervised by the royal organization that was founded in 1975, there are eight industrial cities, namely in Riyadh, Jeddah, Dammam, Quassim, Al-Ihsa'a and Makkah. They have all facilities and services. The Ministry of Industry and Electricity has declared plans to construct new industrial cities in other areas of the kingdom.

— The volume of manpower in the kingdom reached seven million workers, 2.5 million of which are Saudi nationals.

The Agricultural Sector

The agriculture sector in the kingdom plays an important role in the national economy because it is one of the most important economic productive sectors. The developmental policies and plans carried out by the kingdom accomplished an entire agricultural increase, represented in achieving self-sufficiency for the country in agriculture, especially wheat, dates, vegetables, some types of fruits, dairy products, eggs, poultry, fish, and shrimp as well as exporting the surplus of these products to the world markets.

The following figures show the volume of development achieved by the agricultural sector in the kingdom:

— The cultivated land increased from 600 thousand hectares in 1980 to 1.6 million hectares in 1992.

— Nearly 2.9 million hectares of fallow land were distributed to farmers and agricultural companies, of which about 110,128 investors were involved. Until the end of 1998, 6,929 thousand hectares were distributed in accordance with the uncultivated land system, released in 1388 H (1968).

— The Agricultural Bank, established by the country in 1962, offered loans to farmers and investors in the fields of agricultural and animal production, reaching, until the end of 1997, more than SR 29.5 billion. These loans resulted in the installation of more than 3,132 projects specialized in producing vegetables, fruits, dairy products, and meat. The bank also offered aid for production input, agricultural machines and equipment, reaching, from their start in 1973 until the end of 1997, more than SR 10.9 billion. These states bear 50 percent of the value of irrigation machines and 45 percent of the value of the agricultural equipment, tools, and fertilizers.

— The General Corporation for Crops Cells and Flour Grinders established ten industrial complexes in the area of agricultural production in the kingdom to store cereals, production of flour and manufacture of forage. The capacity of storing reached 2.38 million tons and the capacity of flour grinders' production increased to 1.6 million tons.

— The kingdom achieved self-sufficiency in wheat in 1985 and started to export it to the world markets in 1986. The rate of wheat production in the kingdom reached its highest rate in 1992 as it reached 4.2 million tons. But, in order to rationalize the consumption of water and maintain the artisan water, the production was decreased gradually only to meet the self-sufficiency needs of the nation. Exporting wheat came to a halt with the last quantity exported in 1995. A similar action was taken for barley, which had reached its peak of production in 1994 with a quantity of 1.82 million tons and was decreased in 1996 to 464 thousand tons.

— The kingdom's production of vegetables in 1998 reached 2.7 million tons and fruit production reached 1.2 million tons, 648 thousand tons of which were in dates. The production of dairy products reached more than 883 thousand tons and the production of table eggs reached about 2,500 million eggs. The production of hens reached 451 thousand tons and the production of red meat reached 157 thousand tons. Also the production of fish increased to reach 55 thousand tons.

— The rate of annual growth for the agricultural sector reached 8.4 percent during the period from 1969 to 1996 and its participation in the total domestic output in 1998 reached SR 34 billion.

Oil Sector

Although oil plays an important role in the Saudi economy, the government recognized at the beginning that it must not depend on it as a major source of income. Thus, the government worked on developing other income sources, which led to the decrease of the oil private sector participation in the total domestic output to 36 percent. The Saudi Aramco [sic] company, which is one of the largest companies of its type in the world, takes over operations of research, excavation, extraction, refining, and marketing of oil. The latest oil discoveries in the middle led to increasing the kingdom's reserve of oil and gas, which is estimated to be 25 percent of the world's reserves. The kingdom's raw oil production reaches eight million barrels daily. Nine refineries fulfill the country's needs of oil byproducts, which amount to about 1.8 million barrels daily.

The Metallurgical Sector

Efforts exerted in the research and excavation of metals resulted in discovering several sites rich in raw materials. The Ministry of Petroleum and Metal Wealth granted 841 licenses for exploiting granite, marble, limestone, sand, and pottery in addition to granting seventeen concessions to exploit cement, gold, basic metals, and industrial metals. Another fifteen discovering licenses and twenty-six exploring metal licenses were granted.

The production of gold from Gold Cradle and Sukhairat mines reached 150 thousand ounces. The Arab Saudi Metallurgy Company was established in accordance with a royal decree in 1997 as a joint-stock company with a capital of SR four billion. It takes over the development and improvement of the metallurgical industry in the kingdom. Annexed to it are the Gold Cradle project and the Saudi Company for precious metals, which produces gold in the Sukhairat area in Qassim. It seeks to head toward other metallurgical projects, either independently or by sharing in the enterprise with the Saudi private sector or foreign companies. It is worth mentioning that the metallurgical sector in the kingdom plays an important role in the Saudi economy through the projects and companies that presently exist such as the Cement, Gypsum, and Marble Company and other companies that depend on various metal resources. The annual average growth rate in the metallurgical sector is estimated at nine percent and its contribution to the total domestic output at four percent.

Banking Sector

The ten commercial bank services cover various areas of the kingdom through 1,194 branches. They participated, and still participate, in serving the private sector and organizing the circulation operations of shares of the joint-stock companies working in the kingdom under the auspices of the Saudi Monetary Agency. These banks do their work in an active investment atmosphere in addition to the stability of the Saudi riyal exchange rate. Banks in the kingdom use the most modern banking technologies in the world, such as using electronic transference mechanisms for balances and circulation of shares. Electronic money tellers number 1,942, serving more than 4.5 million electronic issue cards for the clients.

The data available on performance of the banks in 1998 show that good performance of these banks continues and their different commercial transactions expand. The net value of loans these banks granted in 1998 reached SR 160.9 billion, with an increase at a rate of 24 percent compared to 1997. The volume of deposits reached R 276.5 billion with an increase at a rate of 7.1 percent compared to last year. As for the net benefits these banks achieved in 1998, they reached about SR 7.28 billion compared to SR 6.6 billion in 1997.

Banks continued supporting their monetary foundation as their capital and reserves increased during the first ten months in 1999, with a ratio of 4.7 percent to reach SR 42.1 billion at the end of October 1999. Thus, the rate of capital sufficiency reached 21.1 percent, which exceeds the international standards by two digits and a half.

In addition to the strength of the banking sector and the kingdom's occupation of four seats of the first ten in the list of the biggest 100 Arab banks, the Saudi market witnessed a great improvement in the movement of share in 1999 compared to the previous year. The general indicator of shares at the end of 16/12/1999 reached 1,974 points against 1,413 points at the start of the year. This is an increase at a ratio of 39.7 percent. It is to be stated that ninety-six Saudi companies put up a part of their shares for circulation. Non-Saudis are allowed to invest in the Saudi share market. The total value of shares circulated in the domestic share market in 1999 reached SR 39.2 billion representing 349 million shares.

ENDNOTE

1. Editor's note: According to the 2005 *Time Almanac*, 2003 estimates of GDP/PPP for Saudi Arabia was U.S. $286.2 billion, per capita $11,800. Real growth rate was 4.7 percent, inflation 1 percent, and unemployment 25 percent. The kingdom exported a total U.S.$86.53 billion with petroleum accounting for 90 percent.

APPENDICES

Appendix I

Genealogy of the Al Saud[1]

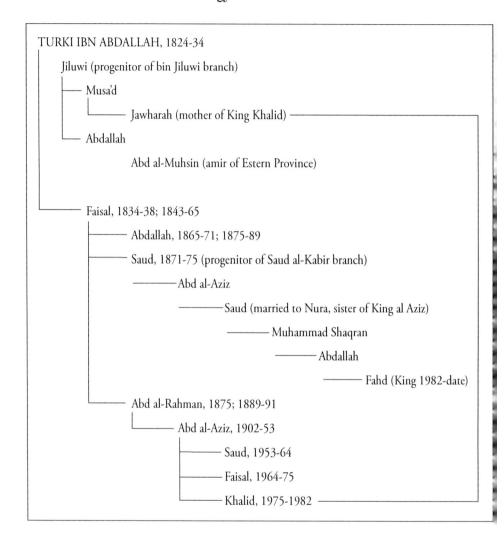

TURKI IBN ABDALLAH, 1824-34

Jiluwi (progenitor of bin Jiluwi branch)

Musa'd

Jawharah (mother of King Khalid)

Abdallah

Abd al-Muhsin (amir of Estern Province)

Faisal, 1834-38; 1843-65

Abdallah, 1865-71; 1875-89

Saud, 1871-75 (progenitor of Saud al-Kabir branch)

Abd al-Aziz

Saud (married to Nura, sister of King al Aziz)

Muhammad Shaqran

Abdallah

Fahd (King 1982-date)

Abd al-Rahman, 1875; 1889-91

Abd al-Aziz, 1902-53

Saud, 1953-64

Faisal, 1964-75

Khalid, 1975-1982

Dates denote periods of rule.
Sources: Adapted from H. StJ. B. Philby, *Arabian Jubilee* (London: Robert Hale, 1952), pp. 250-71; R. Bayly Winder, *Saudi Arabia in the Nineteenth Century* (New York: St. Martin's Press, 1965), p. 279; and David E. Long, *Saudi Arabia*, Washington Papers 39 (Beverly Hills: Sage Publications for the Center for Strategic and International Studies, Georgetown University, 1976), p. 259.

1. From William B. Quandt, *Saudi Arabia in the 1980s,* Washington D.C., The Brooking Institute, 1981, p. 171, reprinted with permission.

Appendix II

Key Members of the Family of King Abd al-Aziz[1]

ABD AL-AZIZ IBN ABD AL-RAHMAN (b. 1880; r. 1902-53; d. 1953

	MOTHER'S NAME
SAUD (b. 1902; r. 1953-64; d. 1969	Wadhba bint Muhammad
FAISAL (b. 1906; r. 1964-75; d. 1975	Tarfah bint al-Shaykh
Abdallah (b. 1921; former minister of interior	Sultana bint Ahmad al-Sudayri
Khalid (b. 1941; governor of Asir)	Haya bint turki bin Jilawi
Muhammad (b. 1937)	Iffat bint Ahmad al-Thunayan
Saud (b. 1941; foreign minister)	Iffat bint Ahmad al-Thunayan
Abd al-Rahman (b. 1942; army officer)	Iffat bint Ahmad al-Thunayan
Bandar (b. 1943; air force)	Iffat bint Ahmad al-Thunayan
Turki (b. 1945; intelligence)	Iffat bint Ahmad al-Thunayan
Muhammad (b. 1910)	Jawharah bint Musa'd bin Jilawi
Khalid (b. 1912; r. 1975-)	Jawharah bint Musa'd bin Jilawi"
Nasir (b. 1920; former governor of Riyadh)	Bazza
Sa'd (b. 1920)	Jawharah bint Sa'd al-Sudayri
Musa'id (b. 1923; his son killed Faisal)	Jawharah bint Sa'd al-Sudayri
Abd al-Muhsin (b. 1925; governor of Medina; "free prince")	Jawharah bint Sa'd al-Sudayri
Fahd (b. 1921; crown prince)	Hussah bint al-Sudayri
Sultan (b. 1924; minister of defense)	Hussah bint al-Sudayri
Abd al-Rahman (b. 1926)	Hussah bint al-Sudayri
Nayif (b. 1933; minister of interior)	Hussah bint al-Sudayri
Turki (b. 1934)	Hussah bint al-Sudayri
Salman (b. 1936; governor of Riyadh)	Hussah bint al-Sudayri
Ahmad (b. 1940; vice-minister of interior)	Hussah bint al-Sudayri
Abdallah (b. 1923; national guard)	Al Fahda bint Asi al-Shuraym
Fawwaz (b. 1934; former governor of Mecca; "free prince")	Bazza
Mish'al (b. 1926; former governor of Mecca; Minister of defense, 1951-56)	Shabida
Mit'ab (b. 1918; minister of public works and Housing)	Shabida
Talal (b. 1931; "free prince")	Munayir
Nawwaf (b. 1934; head of royal palace under Saud)	Munayir
Badr (b. 1933; deputy commander national guard)	Haya bint Sa'd al-Sudyri
Abd al-llah (b. 1935; governor of Qasim)	Haya bint Sa'd al-Sudyri
Abd al-Majid (b. 1940; governor of Tabuk)	Haya bint Sa'd al-Sudyri
Majid (b. 1934; governor of Mecca; former Minister of municipal affairs)	Muhdi
Sattam (b. 1943; deputy governor of Riyadh)	Muhdi
Muqrin (b. 1943; governor of Hail)	Barakah al-Yaminiyah

Sources: Adapted from Brian Lee, *A Handbook of the Al Sa'ud Ruling Family of Saudi Arabia* London; Royal Genealogics, 1980); H. StJ, B. Philby, *Arabian Jubilee* (London: Robert Hale, 1952), pp. 250-71; David E. Long, *Saudi Arabia* Washington Papers 39 (Beverly Hills: Sage publications for the Center for Strategic and International Studies, Georgetown University, 1976), pp. 66-68; "The Royal House of Saud," *Financial Times* (London), March 20, 1978.

1. From William B. Quandt, *Saudi Arabia in the 1980's*, Washington D.C., The Brookings Institution, 1981, pp 172-173, reprinted with permission.

abaya: A black, opaque, floor-length cloak for women when visiting public places or shopping.

Al: Uppercase means "belonging to"; lowercase represents the definite article "the."

Allah: Arabic word for God.

amir (pl., umara): means commander; also means prince.

Awqaf (pl. of waqf): A permanent endowment or trust based on Muslim law for charitable purposes.

fatwa: The basis of a court decision or government action.

hadith: One of the sources of Islamic law based on the precedent of Mohammed's words and deeds.

haram: Sacred and forbidden areas, such as the area surrounding Mecca that is closed to non-Muslims.

hijra (pl. hujar): Means to migrate, to sever relations, or to leave one's tribe. In Saudi Arabia, hijra also refers to the agricultural settlements of the Ikhwan al Muslimin that combine features of religious missions, farming communities, and army camps.

ibn: Means "son of" and is used before a proper name to indicate descent from; "int" means "daughter of."

Ikhwan al Muslimin: The Muslim Brethren.

Iman: Means the leader of congregational prayer.

jihad: Means holy war, the struggle to establish the law of God on earth.

Koran or Quran: Muslims' most sacred book, divided into 114 chapters called "suras." This is the book containing a series of revelations from God to Prophet Mohammed.

majlis: Tribal council (the legislative assembly); also could mean the audience of the king or sheik that is open to all subjects (citizens).

Mecca: The prophet Mohammed required the faithful to make a pilgrimage here once in their lives.

Medina: Another holy site in Saudi Arabia, where Mohammed was buried.

mufti: Religious police; interpreter of Muslim law.

prayer: All Muslims face Mecca as they pray.

qadi: Judge in sharia law courts.

Saudi Calendar: It is called the Hijra, which marks the year the Prophet Mohammed migrated from Makkah to Medina in July 16, 682 A.D./C.E. Based on the lunar year, the Hijra year is shorted than the Western calendar year by eleven days.

Saudi Emblem: The emblem of Saudi Arabia is a palm tree over two crossed swords. The palm tree symbolizes growth and prosperity; and the swords indicate power and valor.

Saudi Flag: The flag of the kingdom is green and rectangular. It carries the inscription: "There is no God but the [one] God. And Mohammed is the Messenger of God." Beneath the inscription is an unsheathed Arabian sword with its handle pointing toward the flagpole. The inscription and the sword are in white.

Saudi Holidays: The kingdom has two major holidays (Eids) every year. The Eid Al-Fitr, which marks the end of the fasting month of Ramadan, starts with a large prayer gathering and then includes visits to relatives and friends. Gifts are usually given to children and close family members. The other holiday, Eid Al-Adha, forms the culmination of the Hajj pilgrimage.

Saudi National Anthem: The text is as follows: "Hasten towards glory and prominence; Glorify the Creator of the heavens; And hoist the green fluttering banner; Displaying the luminous testimony. "Allah is Great, O my homeland; Long live my homeland; A source of pride for Muslims. Long live the King, to safeguard the flag and the homeland."

Saudi National Day: September 23, marking the formal foundation of the kingdom in 1932.

Saudi riyal (SR): The Saudi monetary unit is the riyal, made up of 100 halalas. Notes are in 1, 5, 10, 20, 50, 100, 200, and 500 riyal denominations. The exchange rate has been fixed at U.S. $1=SR 3.75.

Saudi working hours: Government offices are open from 7:30 a.m. to 2:30 p.m. and banks from 8:00 a.m. until noon and 4:00 p.m. to 6:30 p.m., Saturday to Wednesday.

Saudi special rules: Only men are allowed to drive. All the international chains and independents have cars available for rent. Taxis and limousines are widely available.

Saudi transport: The kingdom is served by three international airports at Riyadh, Jeddah, and Damman, as well as several regional carriers. The three major airports are served by carriers from around the world. The towns and cities are well connected by a 162,000 km network of roads. The Saudi Arabian Public Transport Company (SAPTCO) runs a fleet of modern, air-conditioned buses with routes to all major cities and towns. The railway between Riyadh and Dammam has several daily departures.

Saudi visa: A transit visa covers three days and is issued only if it can be proven that you could not get to your destination without traveling through Saudi Arabia. For business purposes, a visiting visa is therefore mandatory. Permanent residents can invite family members for visits on a limited basis. Some tourist visas are available. One must consult the Saudi Arabian Embassy in Washington, D.C., for information.

Saudi time zone: The kingdom is within one time zone, three hours ahead of GMT. Prayer times across the country vary however, because of the differences in the timing of sunrise and sunset.

Saudi world role: The kingdom is a founding member of the Gulf Cooperation Council (GCC). It is also a charter member of the Organization of Petroleum Exporting Countries (OPEC), the United Nations, League of Arab States, Organization of the Islamic Conference, the Organization of Arab Exporting Countries, the World Bank and International Monetary Fund. It is a major provider of aid to developing countries, ranking next to the U.S. in overall assistance.

Sharia: Islamic law as set by the Prophet Mohammed. (Also spelled sharee'ah.)

sharif: Descent from Mohammed through his daughter Fatima.

shaykh: Leader or chief. (Also spelled sheik.)

Shiite: A member of the smaller or the two great divisions of Islam; they believe Ali, Mohammed's cousin and son-in-law, had been designated by Mohammed as his successor.

SR: Saudi riyal.

Sunni: The larger of the two great divisions of Islam. They have no central doctrinal authority but adhere to practices and laws traceable by tradition to Mohammed.

Ulama (sing., alim): Collective term for Muslim religious scholars.

Wahhabi: Name used to designate adherents to Wahhabism by Westerners. Wahhabism is a puritanical concept of Unitarianism—that is, the oneness of God—that was preached by Muhammed ibn Abd al Wahhab, and is practiced by Saudi Arabians.

Appendix IV

Information Resources
For more information, check out these resources:

Al-Riyadh (press)
1155 15th St. NW
Washington, D.C. 20005
Tel. 202-822-0814

Arab News
1535 N. Taylor Street
Arlington, VA 22207
Tel. 703-516-4837
www.arabnews.com

Exchange Arrangements & Exchange Restrictions (annual)
International Monetary Fund
700 19th Street NW
Washington, D.C. 20431
Tel. 202-623-7000
www.imf.org

National Trade Data Bank (monthly)
U.S. Department of Commerce
14th Street and Constitution Ave. NW
Washington D.C. 20230
Tel. 202-482-2000
www.commerce.gov

OECD Economic Outlook (semiannual)
Organization for Economic Cooperation & Development
2001 L Street, NW #650
Washington, D.C. 20036
Tel. 202-785-6323
www.oecdwash.org

Saudi Arabian Embassy Information Bulletin (monthly)
601 New Hampshire Ave. NW
Washington, D.C. 20037
Tel. 202-337-4076
www.saudiembassy.net

Saudi Press Agency
601 New Hampshire Ave. NW
Washington, D.C. 20037
Tel. 202-944-3890
www.spa.gov.sa

World Factbook (annual)
Central Intelligence Agency
Washington Office for Public Information
200 Independence Ave. SW, #314 G
Washington, D.C. 20505
Tel. 703-482-7677
www.cia.gov

World Trade Online
1225 S. Clark Street, #1400
Arlington, VA 22202
Tel. 703-416-8539
www.insidetrade.com

ACKNOWLEDGMENTS

Permission to reprint the following copyright materials is gratefully acknowledged:

Chapters 1-6 of this Reader, from Benson Lee Grayson, *Saudi-American Relations,* (Lanham, Md., University Press of American, 1982, pp. 1-63.

Chapters 9 and 10, from Ragali El Mallakh and Dorothea H. El Mallakh, eds., *Saudi Arabia: Energy, Developmental Planning, and Industrialization,* (Lexington, MA, Lexington Books, 1982, pp. 93-105).

Chapter 11, from the *Washington Post,* November 28, 1981.

Chapter 12, from the *Christian Science Monitor,* July 17, 1981.

Chapter 13, from the *New York Times,* January 21, 1982.

Chapter 14, from the *New York Times,* January 31, 1982.

Chapter 15, from the *Washington Post,* November 28, 1981.

Chapter 16, from the *Christian Science Monitor,* December 21, 1981.

Chapter 17, from the *Christian Science Monitor,* July 17, 1981.

Chapter 19, from the *New York Times,* January 26, 1982.

Chapter 20, from the *Christian Science Monitor,* December 30, 1981.

Chapter 21, from *Washington Post Book World,* January 31, 1982.

Chapter 22, from the *Christian Science Monitor,* January 4, 2004.

Chapter 23, from the *Christian Science Monitor,* January 8, 2004.

Chapter 24, from the *New York Times,* June 19, 2004.

Chapter 25, from the *New York Times,* June 24, 2004.

Chapter 26, from the *Associated Press,* April 25, 2004.

Front cover photography from U.S. Government Archives. Back cover photography by May-Lee Chai.

ABOUT THE
UNIVERSITY OF INDIANAPOLIS PRESS

The University of Indianapolis Press is a nonprofit publisher of original works, specializing in, though not limited to, topics with an international orientation. It is committed to disseminating research and information in pursuit of the goals of scholarship, teaching, and service. The Press aims to foster scholarship by publishing books and monographs by learned writers for the edification of readers. It supports teaching by providing instruction and practical experience through internships and practica in various facets of publishing, including editing, proofreading, production, design, marketing, and organizational management. In the spirit of the University's motto, "Education for Service," the Press encourages a service ethic in its people and its partnerships. The University of Indianapolis Press was institutionalized in August 2003; before its institutionalization, the University of Indianapolis Press published thirteen books, eight of which were under the auspices of the Asian Programs. The Press had specialized in Asian Studies and, as part of its commitment to support projects with an international orientation, will continue to focus on this field while encouraging submission of manuscripts in other fields of study.

BOOKS FROM THE
UNIVERSITY OF INDIANAPOLIS PRESS
(1992–2003)

1. Phylis Lan Lin, Winston Y. Chao, Terri L. Johnson, Joan Persell, and Alfred Tsang, eds. (1992) *Families: East and West.*

2. Wei Wou (1993) *KMT-CCP Paradox: Guiding a Market Economy in China.*

3. John Langdon and Mary McGann. (1993) *The Natural History of Paradigms.*

4. Yu-ning Li, ed. (1994) *Images of Women in Chinese Literature.*

5. Phylis Lan Lin, Ko-Wang Mei, and Huai-chen Peng, eds. (1994) *Marriage and the Family in Chinese Societies: Selected Readings.*

6. Phylis Lan Lin and Wen-hui Tsai, eds. (1995) *Selected Readings on Marriage and the Family: A Global Perspective.*

7. Charles Guthrie, Dan Briere, and Mary Moore. (1995) *The Indianapolis Hispanic Community.*

8. Terry Kent and Marshall Bruce Gentry, eds. (1996) *The Practice and Theory of Ethics.*

9. Phylis Lan Lin and Christi Lan Lin. (1996) *Stories of Chinese Children's Hats: Symbolism and Folklore.*

10. Phylis Lan Lin and David Decker, eds. (1997) *China in Transition: Selected Essays.*

11. Phylis Lan Lin, ed. (1998) *Islam in America: Images and Challenges.*

12. Michelle Stoneburner and Billy Catchings. (1999) *The Meaning of Being Human.*

13. Frederick D. Hill. (2003) *'Downright Devotion to the Cause': A History of the University of Indianapolis and Its Legacy of Service.*

For information on the above titles or to place an order, contact:
University of Indianapolis Press
1400 East Hanna Avenue / Indianapolis, IN 46227 USA
(317) 788-3288 / (317) 788-3480 (fax)
lin@uindy.edu / http://www.uindy.edu/universitypress

NEW TITLES FROM THE
UNIVERSITY OF INDIANAPOLIS PRESS
(2004–2005)

1. brenda Lin. *Wealth Ribbon: Taiwan Bound, America Bound.*

2. May-lee Chai. *Glamorous Asians: Short Stories and Essays.*

3. Chiara Betta. *The Other Middle Kingdom: A Brief History of Muslims in China* (in Chinese and English). Translated by Phylis Lan Lin and Cheng Fang.

4. Phylis Lan Lin and Cheng Fang. *Operational Flexibility: A Study of the Conceptualizations of Aging and Retirement in China* (in Chinese and English). Translated by Phylis Lan Lin and Cheng Fang.

5. Alyia Ma Lynn. *Muslims in China* (in Chinese and English). Translated by Phylis Lan Lin and Cheng Fang.

6. Philip H. Young. *In Days of Knights: A Story for Young People.*

7. James C. Hsiung. *Comprehensive Security: Challenge for Pacific Asia.*

8. Winberg Chai. *Saudi Arabia: A Modern Reader.*

9. Au Ho-nien. *Journey with Art Afar.* Catalog for the Au Ho-nien Museum, University of Indianapolis.